PRAISE F

WILDFIRE: MI!
*AND MADNE**

"A compelling and insightful read regarding the highs and lows of living with schizoaffective disorder. A fascinating and immersive memoir which offers insights beyond what the purely medical model can offer. This is an inspiring and informative read for everyone: medical professionals, caregivers, and those living with a mental health condition."

"Darlleniad cymhellol a craff ynglŷn â'r uchelder a'r iseldir o fyw gydag anhwylder affeithiol sgitszoaffective. Memoir diddorol a drochi sy'n cynnig mewnwelediad y tu hwnt i'r hyn y gall y model meddygol yn unig ei gynnig. Mae hwn yn ddarllen ysbrydoledig a llawn gwybodaeth i bawb: gweithwyr meddygol proffesiynol, rhoddwyr gofal, a'r rhai sy'n byw gyda chyflwr iechyd meddwl."

—**Nadia Dolan,** Senior Social Work Practitioner/Approved
Mental Health Professional (AMHP)
*Uwch-Ymarferydd Gwaith Cymdeithasol/Proffesiynol Iechyd
Meddwl Cymeradwy (AMHP)*

"It should be my dear wife Christine writing this as she is a huge fan of Laura Ruth and spent much time encouraging her and watching her defy all the odds to reach what she believed were her God-given goals. However, Christine is facing her own challenges now as she is in care with dementia, and I am thrilled to be able to commend this amazing account of Laura's journey with all its pain, frustrations, tears, and joys. This devastatingly honest story, warts and all, will inspire some suffering with the traumas of mental health issues; it will challenge professionals working in social care and give Christians insights into the massive obstacles that someone with Laura's condition faces on a daily basis. It gives hope to us all to see that nothing is impossible when we encounter and draw on God's grace and embrace his purpose for our lives."

—**John Noble**, Author, Christian Ministry, and Chairman of the UK National Charismatic & Pentecostal Leaders Conference, 1984–2006.

"Laura tells the story of her extraordinary life with warmth and humour. I winced at her impersonal treatment at the hands of mental health services and wondered how many people feel the same. Her insights into mental illness and spirituality are compelling reading for professionals."

—**Dr. Danielle Rhydderch**, Consultant Psychiatrist.

"Laura writes an honest, at times almost painfully honest, account of her life and experiences. We are told about the significant life events that have helped shape her, ranging from her childhood memories and love-hate relationship with school, her experiences as a missionary, and her career as a statutory social worker.

"At times the tale is a stark one, documenting dark periods of poor mental health and the struggle of trying to balance poor mental health with a sense of deep spirituality. The impact of living with voices and visions is described, and themes of shame and forgiveness are examined. However, at all times, the narrative remains positive and reflective, with flashes of humour. It is an engaging and insightful read for anyone with an interest in mental health and spirituality, and for social work and social care students."

—**Dr. Jo Redcliffe**, Associate Professor of Social Work at Swansea University.

Wildfire: Mission and Madness

by Laura Ruth

© Copyright 2021 Laura Ruth

ISBN 978-1-64663-496-5

All rights reserved. No part of this publication may be reproduced, stored in a retrieval system, or transmitted in any form or by any means—electronic, mechanical, photocopy, recording, or any other— except for brief quotations in printed reviews, without the prior written permission of the author.

Cover art by Laura Ruth

Published by

◤ köehlerbooks™

3705 Shore Drive
Virginia Beach, VA 23455
800-435-4811
www.koehlerbooks.com

LAURA RUTH

WILDFIRE

MISSION AND MADNESS

VIRGINIA BEACH

CAPE CHARLES

TABLE OF CONTENTS

Pilgrims

DEDICATIONS

I WOULD LIKE TO DEDICATE this book to three groups of people.

To my wonderful daughter, Blaze Tallulah. I want to especially thank you for your uniqueness and, although our relationship has not been conventional, you are still here beside me. I want you to know that you are the best and most precious gift God has blessed me with. I am enjoying watching you grow and develop into a mighty woman, a firebrand of love, passion, and beauty.

To all those who have been with me through the journey we call life. To Christine Noble, mentor and encourager. To all those who have been with me for a season and those who are a constant companion. I am grateful to you all; the impact you have had has been transforming. Although at times it has been painful, great things have come forth.

To all those who are yet to come. It will be amazing!

ACKNOWLEDGEMENTS

TO THOSE WHO CONTRIBUTED TO Chapter Four.

Blaze Tallulah Roper

Barbara Meier

Sue Evans

Thank you all for your honest reflections in telling your story of the challenges you have faced in the differing nature of our relationships. Thank you for sticking with me through the tough times, as well as the good. I am so blessed to have you in my life. I am glad to be able to call you "friends."

To *Rethink Mental Illness*. For the permission granted to include the factsheet on schizoaffective disorder.

Life in the Tempest

INTRODUCTION

"The voices may not be real, but they do have some good ideas!"

Unknown

THIS BOOK HAS BEEN WRITTEN during the first lockdown of the Coronavirus pandemic of 2020. Quarantine has provided me with time to reflect, and caused me to ask myself the question, "How did I get here?"

Wildfire: Mission and Madness is a personal story of my life, my work, and my so-called mental illness, that being schizoaffective disorder. Schizoaffective disorder is a combination of experiencing symptoms of both schizophrenia and bipolar. I wanted to write this book to be able to share with you, the reader, in a way that is honest, that does not dramatize situations but exposes the bare truth and reality of learning to live with a severe and enduring mental health condition. I hope I have lifted the lid on some key issues.

This will potentially be a challenge for me, as I am not known for being the most open of books, so to speak. In fact, I am told by those close to me that one of my most annoying traits is my "omission" in communicating with others, be it the small things or with regards to larger issues. My daughter tells me off for it these days. She tells me it "unnerves people," as they wonder what secrets I hold, and there is an air of mystery around me. She says that information out of the blue and surprises are "not good," as it makes others suspicious and does not help in building an open and healthy relationship; it creates distance.

As you read through my story and become aware of the issues I seek to address, you will note many flaws in my character, not only in who I am, but also in what I do and have done. My hope is threefold:

1) Despite my flaws, my faults, and my limitations, it is my hope that you will be encouraged.

2) Despite all our own individual challenges, it is my hope that some may be stirred to live life to the fullest, to rise up, breaking through the barriers, smashing down the walls that imprison us, and throw off the constraints that rob us from all that life has coming our way. Life in the tempest is not easy—it can be extremely scary—but we must go deeper if we are to enter into the fullness of life.

3) It is my hope that a spark will be ignited and fanned into flame, rising up as a mighty fire that will sweep across the landscape of that which we define as "mental illness," seeing new growth coming to life amongst the ashes.

Furthermore, I aim to speak from the heart. I do not seek to provide a professional, social, academic, or biblical-based guidance in my work. Providing the reader with an understanding of issues of the law, policies, and guidance or theological insights is not my undertaking. I am just telling my story and sharing some thoughts I have.

I have tried to tell my story in a language that non-professionals can grasp, but I hope that the experiences and perspectives I share, as a social worker, will be of value to others working in the sector, and to Christians needing insight into mental health problems. I have written this book for all out there like me who have been afflicted with periods of mental illness in their life. It is my hope it would encourage the readers, whoever they may be, and that it will cause others to talk and bring issues into the open without shame or fear.

I have attempted to not only tell my story but to address what I believe to be key issues in learning to live with a severe and enduring mental illness—key issues in the recovery process from that illness—and key issues that those with this form of illness face, be it experiences along their journey or the false beliefs, attitudes, and mysteries surrounding mental illness. I will share with you stories from the mission field during my twenty years of international travels while serving others in the midst of disaster and extreme situations. In doing so, I will tell you about the highs and lows in my relationships and in my work. We will hear from others who have been with me through the good times and the bad. I have defined my own mental illness and I will speak of what it is like to live as a "voice hearer." I will lift the lid on my experience of life inside a psychiatric hospital. I will consider the interface between mental health and spirituality. I aim to present my own thoughts on the challenges I have faced and suggest what factors I believe have been instrumental in seeing change and new life spring up. As I have been challenged, I hope you will be stirred and challenged, too.

I have done some crazy things in my life, but I believe that there are some things in this world that take a mad person to do them or they would just not get done!

The majority of the artwork featured in this book was undertaken by me during the three years between my hospital admissions, that is, between 2011 and 2013. Paintings entitled *Looking In* and *Finding Freedom* I undertook in 1992. Others were painted during the COVID-19 pandemic during lockdown. Chapter Five features a painting titled *She Wants to be Amongst the Stars*. It was painted by my daughter, Blaze.

Looking In

Finding Freedom

CHAPTER ONE
WHO AM I?

"We were born to make history."

Unknown

TO START WITH, A BIT OF HISTORY.

MY ANCESTRY IS AN INTERESTING one on the maternal side. For many years, my aunt has been researching the family tree. She traced the line of my grandfather back to the fifteenth century and has discovered we have noble blood.

We are direct descendants of King Edward IV of the Plantagenet dynasty and House of York (1442–1483): Edward is my fifteenth great-grandfather through the line of Watson. Daughter of King Edward IV and his wife, Elizabeth Woodville, Lady Margaret Watson Plantagenet (1479–1528) was my fourteenth great-grandmother and she married John Watson.

Personally, I have my doubts about the royal connection because, while reading the history of King Edward IV, I cannot find in the list of children a "Margaret" who married a "Watson" who lived into adulthood, be it a legitimate child or in the list of acknowledged "bastards." However, there are genealogists whose opinions would verify my aunt's research. Should this be true, it makes fine reading and stories that are interesting to tell, so let's go with the flow for the sake of argument as it is a family tale they lay claim to!

Deeper

Firestorm

Should this royal connection be true, here are the stories of family members including

King Edward V; King Edward IV; King Richard III; George, Duke of Clarence; and Margaret Pole, the Countess of Salisbury. The story of John Watson, the Bishop of Winchester, a clear ancestor, also follows.

Lady Margaret's brother was named as Prince of Wales in 1471 and later became King Edward V (1470–1483). The twelve-year-old Edward V's reign was brief—from 9th April 1483 to 25th June 1483. He mysteriously disappeared as his Uncle Richard lay claim to the throne. The theory is that Edward V and his brother Richard were murdered by King Richard III, smothered to death with their pillows. William Shakespeare's play *Richard III* makes mention of this tale. Years later, the bones of two children were discovered in the stairway at the Tower of London are believed to be those of the boys.

King Edward IV was victorious in many battles as a "capable and charismatic military commander, who led from the front." Also described as "of heart courageous" and "adventurous." He reigned as King of England twice, with a year out while in exile. His reign was one of two halves, one of war which included the Battle of Towton which was fought in a snowstorm and is said to have been the bloodiest battle ever to take place on English soil. The other half was cultural, economic, political, and diplomatic in nature.

Through his daughter, Elizabeth of York, he was an ancestor of both Tudor and Stuart monarchs, his grandson King Henry VIII being one of them.

Edward IV loved to spend his money on fine clothes, jewels, furnishings, buildings, and historical and literary manuscripts; he spent large amounts on expensive status symbols. He took on the major project of rebuilding St. George's Chapel at Windsor Castle, where in 2018 Prince Harry and Meghan Markle got married before the cameras of the world. He was far from a saver; upon his death, he left a sum of less than £1,200 in the bank belonging to the Crown.

On the website "History Extra", King Edward IV was also allegedly one for the women, bedding numerous ladies and fathering many children. One commentator states that, from her research and contemporary evidence, in his private life King Edward IV was in a same-sex relationship with Henry Beaufort, Duke of Somerset. Apparently this was not unusual; King Edward II and Richard the Lionheart before him also had same-sex intimate relationships.

King Edward IV had two brothers, George Plantagenet 1st Duke of Clarence (1449–1478) and King Richard III (1452–1485). George is said to have played an important role in the War of the Roses. Brother

Richard was the last of the kings of England to die in battle. He died at the Battle of Bosworth fighting against the armies of Henry Tudor. Richard features in Shakespeare's play stating, "My horse, my horse, my kingdom for my horse." George is also a subject and appears as a character in two of Shakespeare's plays, *Henry VI, Part 3* and *Richard III*, where he is portrayed as weak-willed and changeable as evidenced by his continual changing of sides between the House of York and Lancastrians. Additionally, he had an unusual death.

King Edward IV had George arrested and committed to the Tower of London for the crime of treason. He was executed by drowning at the Tower on 18th February 1478, allegedly drowned in a butt of Malmsey wine. On King Edward IV's part, this was a joke referring to his favourite drink. In reading about George, commentators describe his mental health as "never stable." He had the notion and was convinced that one of his wife's ladies-in-waiting poisoned her, resulting in her death. He had her hanged. George's wife, however, had not been poisoned; historians believe she died of either consumption or childbed fever.

Our said cousin of old, Margaret Pole, Countess of Salisbury (1473–1541), daughter of George, Duke of Clarence, was one of only two women in the sixteenth century in England to be a peer in her own right, not through marriage. She was the fifth richest peer in England. Given by King Henry VII, Margaret was married to Sir Richard Pole, a Welshman, in an attempt to reinforce the alliance between the houses of Lancaster and York, thus bringing the houses together and reuniting the land. This marriage was to later feature in one of William Shakespeare's plays. Like her father before her, Margaret met her end at the Tower of London. Prior to her death, Margaret was one of the ladies-in-waiting for Catherine of Aragon, wife of Arthur, Prince of Wales, and after Arthur's death became the first wife of King Henry VIII. Margaret was in and out of favour in the Royal Courts. Margaret was taken to the Tower of London and held there for two and a half years. She was attended to by servants during this time. A poem was carved into her cell wall that reads:

For traitors on the block should die;
I am no traitor, no, not I!
My faithfulness stands fast and so,
Towards the block I shall not go!
Nor make one step, as you shall see;
Christ in Thy Mercy, save Thou me!

However, King Henry VIII ordered her execution. As she was of noble birth, she was not executed in front of a crowd. A low wooden block had been prepared. It is reported that the main executioner was not present that day, off elsewhere in the country on business. Margaret refused to lay her neck on the block as she did not consider herself to be a traitor, and she instructed the young stand-in executioner to take her head any which way he could. Needless to say, she was hacked at with the axe around her head and shoulders, and a swift professional job was far from the case. She is buried within the Tower grounds in the chapel of St. Peter ad Vincula.

Her son, Reginald Pole, later became the last Catholic Archbishop of Canterbury. Margaret was also a Catholic, and in 1886 Pope Leo XIII beatified her as a martyr of the Catholic Church.

This year (2020), the Royal Mint has commissioned a collection of coins based on the Tower of London. I was intrigued to see in their album the mention of cousin Margaret, the Countess of Salisbury. Under the section entitled "Things that go Bump in the Night," I quote, "Unsurprisingly the Tower has earned a reputation as one of Britain's most haunted places. Ann Boleyn, Lady Jane Gray, Edward V and even an apparition of a grizzly bear are said to stalk its grounds. And those bloodcurdling screams in the dead of night? They are said to be the wailings of the Countess of Salisbury as she tries to break free from the executioner's grip and avoid his spectral axe."

One further ancestor of note is the Bishop of Winchester, John Watson (1520–1584), my twelfth great-grandfather. He was educated at Oxford University and graduated as a Doctor of Medicine. John Watson paid to the 1st Earl of Leicester, Robert Dudley, £200 to lobby for him NOT to be made a bishop. The Earl in turn spoke with Queen Elizabeth I, who was on the throne at that time, informing her of his £200 request. Her response: "Nay, then, Watson shall have it, who will give 200 pound to decline, than he who will give 2,000 pound to attain it." The Queen bestowed the position of bishop upon him. John Watson is buried in Winchester Cathedral in the north side of the nave in the fifth bay. The inscription on his burial stone is written in Latin, and it translates ". . . a very wise father. A very good man, tender especially towards the Needy . . ."

Otherwise, on the maternal side of the family, according to my mother, they were all either in prison or in the lunatic asylum. There were children born out of wedlock and were the products of shenanigans between upstairs and downstairs at a country manor. All I can say is, what a bunch! As for my father's side of the family, I do not know.

So why a bit of history to kick us off? Firstly, I do confess, I love history. I find it both gripping and fascinating. Secondly, this book is a story of my journey through life and learning to live with mental illness. A search for meaning, causes, triggers—the root and understanding of how I came to develop a severe mental health condition—has been something my mind has often pondered upon. Commentators on mental health largely attribute the possible causes in five categories: genes and the family history; environmental and life experiences; trauma; biological factors such as chemical imbalances in the brain; and finally, the element of mystery and the unexplained. In reflecting on my blood line, it would appear that they are indeed a mad bunch of individuals and if, in my case, genetics has anything to do with it, the history speaks for itself!

SO, TO PRESENT TIMES.

I was born in 1969 in Bournemouth on the south coast of England. I grew up in Poole, Dorset. My playground was Poole Harbour and Sandbanks beach. Poole Harbour is the second largest natural harbour in the world after Sydney, Australia, boasting of five islands contained within. The largest island is Brownsea Island and is owned by the National Trust where Baden-Powell made home to the Scout and Guide movements campout; it is also known for its red squirrels. The Sandbanks beach (area) today has the most expensive real estate in the world, taking over from both Monte Carlo and Miami. There is a tiny stretch of road measuring 850 feet made up of thirteen waterfront mansions totalling £93 million. And no, I have never lived, nor am I ever likely to live, in one of them!

During the summer months of my early years, we practically lived on the beach at Shore Road. Growing up, I was either in or on the water. I swam five nights per week, Monday to Friday, with gala competitions on Saturdays. I loved kayaking and sailing. At one time I was even a junior lifeguard on Sandbanks beach. This love of the water has been a theme throughout my life as I still like to play on the water to this day.

FAMILY COMPOSITION

My mum and dad are Londoners, and I have a younger sister. On my father's side I had a strong bond with my grandmother, Ruth. My grandfather passed away three years before I was born. I have two uncles and four cousins. On my mother's side of the family was my nan and granddad, two aunts and one uncle with six cousins.

Growing up, I felt very close to my paternal grandmother. I was later to take on her Christian name as my surname. I am the eldest of her grandchildren. We would visit her in her London home once a year, with her coming down to visit us during the summer. I loved just being with her. I can remember one summer when, instead of my normal playing out in the street with my friends, I stayed in just to be with her. As a family, we went to the beach with her. It was usual for me to run into the sea, diving in and splashing around, but when my nan came to the shoreline I would instantly go out and hold her hand as we paddled together in the shallows. As I got older, there were a couple of occasions when I travelled alone on public transport to visit her. First, I caught the bus from Poole to London Victoria, then went on the Underground to Seven Sisters where I boarded a train to Edmonton. The first time I made this journey alone

I believe I was eleven years old. It was a great adventure, especially getting across London on the Underground. I'm not sure if in today's world I would send an unaccompanied child on such a trip. Of course, as with many grandmothers, Nan would spoil me rotten. The greatest thing of all, however, was the emotional attachment. She'd always wanted a girl but gave birth to three boys, and then here I was, the first of her grandchildren, a girl. I clearly remember her cooking me fishfinger sandwiches. To this day, it is a comfort food for me. It was our plan that I would go and live with her when I turned sixteen, but she died during my teen years. The funeral was the day before I turned sixteen! Her death hit me hard, and it took me many years to recover from the loss. I was overwhelmed with crippling grief and great sadness. It left such emptiness and incredible pain. My bond with her had been greater than with any other family member.

When I was five, I met my mum's family for the first time. Up until that point I didn't even know they existed. When other children used to brag that they had two nans and granddads, I simply used to say, "So, I have my nan and Uncle Cliff." Uncle Cliff was my grandfather's brother and companion to my nan, often travelling with her on her holidays. I never even wondered or questioned why my mother didn't have any family. One day when we were at my nan's house, I was informed we were going to visit my other nan and granddad. I am told I was quite excited by this, and in meeting them, I went into their house as if this was nothing new and that it had always been. They lived on a council estate that was built following the bombings on London of the Second World War, and they were one of the first families to move in. In their garden was a children's roundabout, just like the ones that are in the park, and a "swimming pool" which my granddad had built himself. I think it felt like a swimming pool due to my age and height, but in reality, it was a paddling pool, although it did have a deep end and a shallow end. There was also an outside toilet which was a novelty to me. Downstairs inside the house, the back room was where everyone used to congregate around an open coal fire. The front room was only used on special occasions and for parties. My granddad had a bar and music equipment in there as he fancied himself as a bit of a DJ. My granddad was definitely the dominant character in that household. My nan was just there. Over the years I didn't feel a particular bond with them and really just saw them as my mother's family rather than my own. Don't get me wrong, there were good times and I had fun playing with my cousins. My cousins were local so they would sometimes come down on their bikes. So that we could go out riding around the estate, Granddad said I could use his bike; he said that he knew I could manage riding his bike and that I was to by no means to allow any of the others to ride it. There were also holidays that were fun. One on the canal was memorable; we went over the aqueduct at Llangollen, but as our parents were in fear and panic due to the sheer drop on one side, they locked us kids inside the boat!

EARLY LIFE

I have fond memories of my young days, not only because much of it was spent on the beach, but also because of the time spent out playing in the street with the other children in my neighbourhood. We would go out on our bikes—the older I got, I went miles from home—and yet somehow we knew when it was time to go home for meals, even though we didn't have a watch between us. A childhood in the '70s gave us freedom to roam and have numerous adventures. I used to collect frogs' spawn and newts, bringing them home and putting them in the pond in our back garden. I also loved fossil hunting on Dorset's Jurassic Coast gaining a fine collection of ammonites and belemnites; in fact, I was awarded my Brownies' Collector badge for it. After one storm I collected one hundred ammonites in one day. Holidays were spent camping in the UK, and when we were home, I used to camp out in the back garden.

On Sundays my mum took us to church. My dad became a Christian when I was eight years old, and from that point on we went to church weekly as a family. When I was twelve, I approached my parents telling them I no longer wished to go to church. They tried to reason with me, but I used my nan as an excuse saying, "She was made to go to church when she was young, she never made you go to church, Dad, and now she hates anything religious." That sealed my ticket to stay home from church. There was one condition, though; I had to attend to the Sunday dinner while they were out, but that was okay with me.

One day I asked my parents if I could have my ears pierced. Their answer was "No, you cannot go to a shop and have your ears pierced." I did hear what they said, so I pierced my own ears. When they saw my pierced ears, they said, "We told you that you couldn't have your ears pierced." I replied, "No, you told me I couldn't go to a shop to have my ears pierced. I didn't go to a shop. I did them myself. Nan pierced her own ears herself, too." That was pretty much the end of that argument. They must have told members of their church house group about it because after a meeting that same evening in our lounge, one of the women came to me offering advice on how to care for my newly pierced ears.

During these younger years I was aware that my mum was often upset. She was deeply affected by the relationship she had with her own family. As I have already said, I did not know my grandparents, aunts, uncles, and cousins on her side of the family until I was five years old. When my mum planned to marry my dad, she was thrown out of her family home. My grandfather would not allow anyone in the family to speak to her, and if one of them saw her, they crossed the street. They did not attend the wedding. When I was five, there was a reunion. However, this was not the last of this type of treatment. There were other occasions where they didn't speak to her or us for years at a time. Understandably, my mum carried the pain of this with her. She would become low in mood and tearful as she tried to work through the emotional upset in its many forms. As a young observer, I was impacted by this, too.

MY TEEN YEARS

In my teenage years my school days didn't particularly go well. They were certainly not the best years of my life. At senior level I opted to go to the local Catholic secondary modern school. I decided I wanted to go there because it was a small school of approximately 400 pupils, and only three from my junior school went there. I did not want to go to the main comprehensive high school in town with everyone else because I had been bullied at times during my time at the middle school, and I wanted to break free from those people and relationships. My first and last years there were okay, but when I was in the third and fourth year it was somewhat chaotic and troublesome.

I started to get in trouble with the teachers on a regular basis. I was often removed from the classroom, and I developed a bit of a reputation. What did I do? Well, that was the thing; I just sat there at the back of the room doing nothing. I wasn't causing trouble, nor was I doing my work. My presence somehow caused others to act up and behave badly. I was told that when I was removed from the class, peace and order returned. Much of my time was spent in corridors and outside the headmaster's office. Teachers would write in my school diary, but my parents didn't see the teachers' comments because I forged my parents' signatures before returning the diary. It wasn't until one day when the school phoned home and invited my parents to a consultation that they discovered what the situation was. Even when my parents were made aware that there were problems—when teachers would phone them to express the challenges they faced with me—my parents would ask "What has she done?" and the answer was always, "Well, nothing, but . . ." As I was not in the classroom anyway, I often decided to play truant. Sometimes I would go in for registration, and then just walk out down the long drive and out through the school gates. Other days I just wouldn't go at all. I hid in trees, went to the park and spent days on the beach.

As far as friendships went, I was friends with everybody and friends with nobody; I got on well with both the boys and the girls, the cool kids and the geeks. One day in the last week of the summer term during an art lesson which was outside, a girl came up to me with a number of other girls around her, wanting a fight. The teacher had gone into the building, and we were out there, unsupervised, drawing the trees in front of us. I put down my pencil and paper and stood up. She was quite a tall girl, or maybe she was average height as I was a small kid. So, a fight began. The whole class jumped up and stood around. We were on a bank, so I made sure I stood uphill. She swung at me as I did at her a couple of times. Her long nails scratched my lip. I tasted a little blood. That was it. When I punched her first in the eye and then swung my fist to hit her on the ear, she yelled out, so I did it again. The fight was over, and she went off inside, crying to the teacher. I had given her a black eye and damaged her ear in some way. No one ever tried it on with me again. The art teacher went absolutely ballistic. He had me in the art room on my own, he was shouting with spit spraying everywhere, he threw tables, and then told me to go to the headmaster's office. My parents didn't get to hear about this until years later—I guess as it was the end of term anyway.

In my options that were to begin after the summer break, I had signed up for O Level Art. The art teacher clearly did not want me in his class. I kept my head down, I did not make eye contact with him, and I did not turn and talk with another pupil while in his classroom. I knew he was watching me and looking for any opportunity to expel me from his classroom and I was not going to give him the satisfaction. When I was painting, he would come up to me, take the paintbrush out of my hand, and say, "Not like that, like this," painting over my work. When it came to the mock exam, he gave me a D. A few months later, it came to the actual O Level Art exam. All the work was sent off to an external examiner. My grade came back as an A. I went to my art teacher because he'd said, prior to the exams, that work would be given back to those who got a grade A; their work would be sent back while the others would be destroyed. He told me my painting had not been returned because it was most likely put in the incinerator, but he did give me a photo of my painting he had taken of all pieces undertaken by the whole class. When he handed me the photo, he asked me where my portfolio was. I told him I didn't have one, and he replied, "Why not? You should be going to art college." I politely said thank you for the photo and walked out that door.

My teen years were the noticeable start of my mental health difficulties. My mood was low, I became depressed, and at times, I felt suicidal. It was also a time when I started hearing voices. The voices were negative and nasty toward me. They attacked my self-esteem. It was like my brain was on fire. I started to harm myself by burning myself with matches. I tried to put my fist through a pane of glass. I hit myself over the head with cooking pots. I wanted to feel physical pain that was greater than the pain I felt inside me, so the physical pain would somehow reduce the emotional pain. It started as an act I was in control of and something I chose to inflict on myself. With the increase of my voices, they started to tell me I needed to hurt myself. I clearly remember one day holding a match to my stomach. The voices told me that it was not good enough to burn my arm as it wouldn't hurt as much, and the skin on my stomach would be more sensitive. I lit a match and placed it on my stomach. It hurt a lot. I tried to pull the match away. I can remember the effort I was putting in to pull the match off, but I couldn't; the voices wouldn't let me. I was no longer in control, they were. They had taken over. I was powerless. Fear came over me. I never spoke to anyone about what was going on and the way I felt. Since that time, there have been occasions where I have been harmed by being burnt. There have been no further times that I have self-harmed when I have chosen to do that to myself. All instances were driven by the voices that have been commanding in nature. Personally, I don't consider that to be self-harm.

There was a night I decided to go out with a group of friends. It was the first time I went out, and the last. We decided to walk to the beach at Branksome. On the way, we walked down an unlit lane that ran parallel with the local psychiatric hospital. We told stories of escaped patients running through the woods as mad axe murderers, frightening ourselves! When we got to the beach, we spent time talking, drinking alcohol, and smoking. When it was time to start the walk home, I called to one of the lads who was in the toilet at the time. He told me to come in and wait for him as he wouldn't be a minute. He came on to me and we kissed. He proceeded by coming on to me strong, and he got me on the floor. The floor was cold, wet, and sandy, and the toilet block stank. He was older than I was. He was tall and strong. He overpowered me and he raped me.

It was like I was lifted out of my own body and, although things were happening to me, I was paralysed and unable to do anything about it. When it was finished, I walked home. I was half an hour late because I was supposed to be back home by 10:30 p.m. and it was nearly 11. My parents told me off for being late. I did not tell them what had happened. In fact, I did not tell anyone for years. That night I did not sleep. I was in pain down below, and there was blood on my knickers. The next morning, I got up and went to school, but I was in pain all day. This experience was not the start of my mental health struggles, but it certainly did not help. My painting *Looking In* depicts how I felt. I saw myself as being locked out of the toy shop, and my childhood was over. It was like there were different parts of me. There is the hurt little girl and there is also the part of me that was trying to fight and did not want to grow up, depicted by the Peter Pan character. There is also the part of me that was mocking me, laughing at me, wanting to make a song-and-dance routine out of the whole situation. The large face on the left of the painting is the face of the lad who attacked me. A couple of years later, I found myself in a situation where I was paired with the same guy in a sailing dinghy for the day. I felt unable to speak up and didn't know how to prevent this pairing. It was a terrible day being stuck alone with him in a boat. We did not speak to each other all day. On the sail back in the afternoon, he was on the tiller, we were sailing close-hauled, I was leaning out of the boat like one should, and he suddenly let the wind out of the sail. I was dragged under the water, unable to get out. When he pulled the sail in again, I came up. He smirked at me. It was like he was telling me he still had the power, and he was in control.

By the end of the fourth year at senior school, I was disillusioned with my life, and I couldn't carry on as I was. I started to go to a mid-week youth group at my parents' church, although still not attending services on Sunday. The youth leaders were going to take some of the group members on a Christian summer camp. I asked if I could go. My parents asked me if I was sure I wanted to go because it would include lots of meetings. I said I did, and they paid for me to go. It was July 1984—my fifteenth birthday—and

I went off to the Youth With A Mission (YWAM) camp. I said to God, *If you are real and can change my life, then I'll give you one week to show yourself to me. Otherwise, forget it.* As I said this to God, I thought I had better give him a fair chance, so I planned to attend all the meetings. I didn't want to go to the youth meetings and activities as I was serious about giving God a proper chance, so instead I went along to all the adult meetings. I sat at the back observing all that was going on, while often standing on the chair so I could get a better view. By the end of the week, I had given my life to Christ. Through a dream, I also felt that God had a purpose for my life, one of missions. I will tell you more about that in Chapter Two. The following week I went on a second camp, a Christian youth activities camp. During the morning Bible study time, I believed God wanted me to be baptized in water. When I came home from camp, I decided that I wanted to go to the church locally where I had met others from the YWAM camp. It was a different church from the one my parents attended. My first Sunday service was to be on a farm, as they were having baptisms in the lake. One day earlier, I went with my dad to the leaders of the church. I told them that I felt God wanted me to be baptized and discussed with them why and what the symbolism and purpose for this was. They agreed, and so that Sunday I was, indeed, baptized in water. There was still four weeks of the summer holidays to go, and I spent much of it in my room reading my Bible. I was working through a daily reading booklet, *Young People's Every Day With Jesus for New Christians.* Day ten was about being "filled with the spirit." I read about gifts that God gives. One of these was "the gift of tongues." I closed my eyes and prayed that God would fill me with his Holy Spirit. The booklet said that it doesn't happen immediately, that you have to wait on God. After I prayed, I was silent and waited. After a few minutes, I opened one eye and looked up. I said out loud, "Is that long enough?" I closed my eyes again and started speaking in tongues. The rest of the summer I spent gaining knowledge of who God, Jesus, and the Holy Spirit were with my Bible, and with new records I had bought of the music of Keith Green, the Christian singer and songwriter who, sadly, died in a plane crash in 1982 at the age of twenty-eight.

Following the summer holidays, I went back to school. A week or so had passed and my mum got a phone call from one of my teachers. Naturally, her heart sank as she thought, *What now?* The teacher said, "I don't understand it. I have never seen it before! How can someone change so much over the holidays? She's a different person." My mood had lifted, and the voices were quiet—at least for now.

YOUNG ADULTHOOD

At age fifteen I came to Wales for the first time. The missionary organisation I joined was based here. Initially, I went for four months, and returned home to gain support from my church in providing me with the funding and to be sent out as their missionary. I returned to Wales at eighteen, never returning home other than to visit. When I arrived at the mission, like all newcomers, I went through a three-month training programme. One of the challenges I remember was, "Are you prepared to be a martyr for the gospel?" I sat there thinking of all the possible ways someone could kill me, and I can tell you my answer was not an immediate "Yes." However, given my new chosen vocation, the concept could become a reality, so it was not an issue to be dismissed.

I became part of a community. We did everything together, living together around the clock seven days a week. Every Thursday was prayer day and then we fasted as well. In May we had a prayer week and December was prayer month which included a three-day fast. Every morning we met together at 8 a.m. for an hour of prayer and worship. For the ten years of my ministry when I worked within that organisation, I had not a clue as to what was happening in the outside world. I did not know of items to hit the news, or popular music, for example. However, I did know all about the Gulf War, as for the duration of that war we prayed 24/7, taking turns in hourly slots day and night. I do confess that, once or twice when it was my house's turn to wake up at 3 a.m. to pray, I pretended to be asleep and didn't get up! Between all the praying, we had jobs. I was assigned to the youth team and became an outdoor pursuit instructor where I particularly enjoyed teaching sailing and kayaking. From Easter through to the end of the summer, we hosted church youth groups that came to us for weekends and week camps, both under canvas and at our residential centre. We also took groups of students on expeditions overseas. I very much enjoyed my time in the mission. I learnt lots about other countries and cultures and was able to go and experience them. During this period, struggles with my mental health started to surface again. I was supported by those around me, and with prayer.

MARRIAGE, MOTHERHOOD AND DIVORCE

At the mission, I met the man who was to become my husband. This new life—it was not in my original plan—all came my way, and I will touch on these at a later point. The greatest change, of course, was being blessed with a daughter. The need to care for her and put her first kept me going through the rough times and the smooth. If I hadn't had her in my life, I don't know how things would have turned out. Having a little life that I was responsible for made me get out of bed in the morning, establish routines, and smile as I watched her grow and develop. She was and remains a source of joy.

WORKING LIFE

For twenty years I was a missionary and a minister. I travelled to a number of places in the world, some of which will show up on my passport, and one or two which will not. There were times where we went "undercover" because certain countries and regions do not allow missionaries within their borders. Those times provided a special sense of excitement. There was an occasion where we wanted to travel in a certain region which I shall not name. We made up our own documents granting us permission to enter. The top of a drinks bottle was used as the stamp, in an attempt to make the documents look official. When we got to the border control manned by military personnel complete with guns, it was slightly nerve wracking waiting to see if our "creative efforts" would be successful. Fortunately for us, they were. Over the years, I have worked in jungles and deserts, I have been caught up in a military coup, and I have worked in a war zone and disaster areas. I loved the adventure.

Much of my work in the UK has also been in the ministry. I have worked in full-time positions in leadership teams within the church and my husband has been the youth pastor. When working as an itinerant minister I preached in many chapels in the valleys of South Wales. One initiative I forged ahead with was serving as the chaplain for two of our local Asda supermarket stores over a three-year period. That was interesting in itself. I was there for both staff and customers. Each Christmas and Easter I would do an in-store mini-service over the loudspeaker and broadcast live throughout the store. Local schoolchildren provided the singing and, on one occasion, the town mayor officially announced the service open, which I found amusing. I used to walk the aisles speaking with customers. There was one chap who instantly told me he was an atheist when I said hello to him, after which he proceeded to tell me his life story and started crying in the baked bean aisle!

As well as working in the Christian ministry, I have had a number of seasonal jobs as a car park attendant, boat yard assistant, Christmas elf, sorting the Christmas post for the Royal Mail, a dinner lady and a teaching assistant in a primary school. I also undertook voluntary work as a Childline Counsellor for three years.

Somehow, and I am not quite sure of the events leading up to it, I applied to go to university in 2004. The course I wanted to enrol in was the post graduate diploma in social work which had an attachment of a master's degree in social sciences. It was to be the last diploma social work course before changing to the undergraduate degree. There were 400 applicants and fifty places. I was invited to interview. Now, you have to bear in mind, I had left school twenty years earlier, I have just one O level and that was in Art, and seven CSEs. I have no A levels, no bachelor degree, and I did not even do an access course. But, they let me in and gave me a place—unbelievable! When the course started, we were "live" so to speak, as each essay was marked as part of our results. I had never written an essay in my life before this point; I really hadn't a clue. Following completion of the Dip SW, my grades were good enough for me to move on and do the masters. There, my dissertation was entitled "Engaging with Children and Communities in Times of Disaster." Out of a class of fifty, twelve of us graduated with our master's degree in the summer of 2008. So, you could say I am a master of disaster!

Despite qualifying as a social worker, I had no intention of working in that field in the UK. I simply wanted the masters as a back-pocket qualification in working overseas, because prior to that I had rubbed shoulders with workers from major humanitarian organisations including the UN and, should it come up, I wanted to be able to say, "I've got one of them, too." However, when my husband left, I was in a situation where I needed the means to provide for my daughter—feed her, keep a roof over her head, and give her opportunities in life that, without resources, she would not have otherwise had. I was therefore forced into a position where I needed to go out to work, so being a social worker was the obvious way ahead, given I had recently had training to be able to do so. For over a decade now, I have been working for social services, first in Child Protection where I worked for eleven years and now for the past three years in the Community Mental Health Team. Working for social services in itself is a bit of a strange one. When I told my friends, a number of them said, "Social services? You? Wouldn't a voluntary organisation be a better match?" I think I wanted to prove to myself that I could be professional, working within strict rules and guidelines, following policies and procedures. I wanted to know if I could do a "proper job." This was something that had eluded me to date as I had been used to winging it and being "creative" in getting results, as well as being my own boss all these years. My first manager was fabulous and our relationship transitioned; she is now someone I call a friend. Supervisions were often long, going through my caseload, and there were plenty of laughs. She often had to get her "red pen" out when marking my assessments. I guess you can say I had a way of writing things that was not considered to be strictly professional, but I thought I had presented the situation so that the client would understand in their own language. Once, in speaking of a mother who had struggles with addiction and wanted to live with her drug dealer boyfriend, I wrote, ". . . it is like a chocoholic moving in with Willy Wonka . . ." Bless my manager, as she had the patience of a saint in working with me, and I did take her to the edge on a number of occasions! She took me under her wing, and I soon learnt how to operate in a professional manner while being myself at same time.

I continue to work for social services to this day, and although the road has not always been easy, I enjoy what I do. I believe I am where I am meant to be at this time.

WHAT IS IN A NAME?

I am a great believer in the importance of names and what they mean. I feel that what we are called is what we will become. My name is Laura Ruth, Laura meaning "laurel wreath—the victor's crown, to be crowned victorious" and Ruth meaning "compassionate." If you put my two names together, I am "Victorious Compassion." It is my hope that I will continue to grow into my name. I feel that my name, Laura, that I was born with, has served me well in that I will overcome and be victorious!

In the Midst of Disaster

Asian Tsunami

CHAPTER TWO
ON A MISSION

"Be fearless in the pursuit of what sets your heart on fire."

Unknown

Take Five!

I HAD JUST HAD MY fifteenth birthday. I was camping. One night I had an extremely vivid dream. I was in my canoe paddling down the Amazon River. I was travelling to the tribe's people to visit them as a missionary. When I awoke, I found myself on my knees shouting out the name of Jesus. It was at that moment I knew God was calling me to missions. It was just three years later that I found myself in Brazil in the Amazon region. In the late '80s and early '90s I travelled to Brazil four times. On two of those trips, I drove from the east coast of Brazil into Bolivia and back again. Over my twenty years working as a missionary, I had the privilege of travelling not only to South America, but also Africa, Asia, and Europe.

Throughout my missionary years, my mental health was somewhat up and down. There were times when I was highly active, full of energy, and the buzz and adrenalin rush was magnificent. Yet there were also times of great depression and despair. During those years, we did not seek professional help. I lived in a community and was supported and cared for by those around me. In the darkest of days, friends took shifts to be with me around the clock, fearing that if I was alone, I would take my own life. As well as being a woman of action, I had a prophetic edge. In my left ear I would hear the voice of God. These were words of encouragement, affirmation, and direction. The insight I received not only came audibly but also in dreams and visions. I would share these with individuals and in meetings. These words were well received and had a positive impact. Yet at the same time, in my right ear, I would hear the voices that, in my youth, I had named "Tom" and "Jerry." These voices were in complete contrast to what I heard in my left ear. They were words that pulled me down; they were destructive and nasty. In nature, they were murderous and spoke of suicide; they were death. I tried to ignore these voices, but they would become loud and shout at me.

My missions have been a significant part of my life and I would like to share some of my stories with you.

SRI LANKA

During those years, I would act on my voices. In fact, I would go as far as saying that I followed my voices around the world into a vast number of situations, and in doing so would take other people with me. I want to make it clear: I never forced anyone to come along. However, on occasions, besides putting myself at risk and in danger, I put the lives of others in danger, too. One day while travelling in the northeast of Sri Lanka in Tamil Tiger territory, we drove through a minefield, albeit on a track, our destination being a remote, cut-off village. While we were in that region, we were being monitored by the Tamil Tigers, a group that some would define as a terrorist organisation. I guess that maybe it was not a smart move on my part to say to a soldier, "You are a little man with a big gun. I want to see the big man." But I did go alone to speak, leader-to-leader, after I got the permissions that I was seeking, and the task at hand was achieved. So, it all worked out for the greater good. It did not occur to me that others were afraid. The thought that I was potentially putting others in harm's way did not cross my mind. I felt an incredible energy pumping through my veins. I felt alive; I felt invincible.

In 2005, I worked for six months during the aftermath of the Asian tsunami in Sri Lanka. At that time, many organisations, global and local, descended on the country to bring aid and relief to the multitudes affected by this natural disaster. Every Friday in Colombo, I attended the multi-agency coordination gathering of leaders and representatives from fifty-plus groups that operated in the field. In working with the affected population and vulnerable people groups, it was important for us not to duplicate what was already being done but instead to look for the gaps, look to see where people were falling through the net. In this way I engaged in a number of small initiatives and projects, ranging from giving aid to facilitating small business start-ups. I am particularly proud of the brick-making project. I was also involved in building houses and connecting a school here in the UK with a school there through a shoe-giving project, to name a few.

It was during this time that the local prison came to my attention. The prison population and staff were affected by the tsunami, but no aid organisations were working in there. I decided to write a somewhat creative letter of introduction to the chief jailer (as they are called in Sri Lanka) with a desire to assist should it be required. Within hours, I received an invitation to go and meet with the chief jailer at the prison. As it happened, I had a group of students from my home university for a few more days. I asked the students if they wanted to come with me as my team. I told them I didn't really know why I was going or what was going to happen when I got there. I also asked one student to take a notebook and pen and, when I turned to her to say something or give her a nod, she should write something down. To be honest, I told my scribe that what she wrote down wasn't really important, but I thought it would look good. She also had a Nationwide Bank pen with her. I asked her to put her thumb over the "wide" bit. Again, I thought it would look the part.

The day arrived and we went to the prison at our given hour. We were given a tour of the prison within the walls in both the main male population housing 800 men and also the smaller female block. We saw the yard, the kitchen, toilet and bathing facilities, the cells, a small room that functioned as a chapel, and the prison hospital. We spoke with a few inmates and saw the official rooms. The chief jailer explained to us what life and living conditions were like in the prison, and we were able to see for ourselves. It was interesting to note that the only place where there were any beds was in the hospital.

In the female block there were mothers with children and babies, and also young teenagers. I engaged the chief, as I was to later call him, in conversation about why children were present. Interestingly, he informed me that the teenagers had been victims of sexual abuse. Yes, you did read that right. They were victims, being housed as unaccompanied minors in an adult prison. The youngest I spoke with was just eleven years old. Officially, there are no children in Sri Lankan prisons. Children go to probation. However, probation sent the children to prison, allegedly on their way to having a medical exam or while in transit to the courts. Both girls and boys pass through the prison on a regular basis, in some cases staying weeks at a time.

The babies there accompanied their mothers. Within my team of students, there was a nurse. The team were standing together near the door while the chief invited me to step forward with him to meet and speak with the women. On being introduced to one lady holding a newborn baby, I asked the chief if I could invite my nurse over to examine the baby. He gave his permission, and I called the nurse over. The baby was beautiful and healthy.

The female compound hosted approximately thirty to forty women. There were two large cells where the women slept on thin mats on the floor at night. The yard was dirt which got muddy when it rained. There was a single tree that provided some shade from the relentless sun and the heat of the day. For bathing, there was a well that the women drew water from to pour over themselves.

It appeared that my creative letter and the inspection of the prison we undertook opened a door. Our team had to fly back to the UK. Over the next ten-week period I went inside the prison twice a week to meet with the chief, and I spent time talking with 10 percent of the prison population, around eighty people. I also built a nursery and fully equipped it, along with providing new toilets in the female block.

The chief himself did not have the authority to allow me to come and go freely within the prison. So, I persuaded him to give me the personal phone number of the head of prisons in the country. Then I phoned him up; he was on the golf course at the time. I advised him which prison I wanted to go in and what I wanted to do. I said that I had been told that I needed his permission, in writing, to do it. I also told him I would be in Colombo, a four-hour drive away, the next morning and would meet him in his office. He agreed. When I got there, I had never been into such a palatial office in all my life. I spoke with him, and he said, "Yes, go ahead and do it." I told him that I was grateful, but I needed permission in writing with his signature, and that I would leave only after he gave it to me. That's what happened. It wasn't until I got in the van to go back down south that it suddenly came over me: What had I just done?

Befriending the chief was an interesting experience. He was in charge; he was the main man. Whatever he said to his staff and the prisoners, there were no questions asked, and on his command, they would run to it. I thought to myself, *the chief is either very well respected as a good man or he is to be feared.* I never did decide which of the two it was, but I do like to see the best in people. However, in my interactions with him, I was aware that I needed to tread carefully. Despite this, I didn't hold back, and I found a way of asking questions to appeal to his important status in order to get the answers I wanted. One day I had read a short statement in the newspaper of a man in the prison who had fallen and died. The article said nothing more than that. I was thinking to myself, *Fell from where? This story doesn't ring true.* The next time I visited with the chief, I found the opportunity to ask him about the incident. He told me the man was in debt for roughly the equivalent of £5. He was in prison because he owed someone money. When he came to the prison from the police station, he had been badly beaten. The chief decided to place this man in the prison hospital. He was there for three days. On the third day, he fell off the bed and died. This incredibly sad story answered my question of where he had fallen from. Another day, the chief wanted to show me his homemade video of the day the tsunami broke through the gates of the prison and caused panic and rioting within its walls. He had already told me that on a previous occasion he had ordered guards to shoot their rifles in an attempt to bring about order, so I wasn't quite sure what I was going to see. Fortunately, no one was being shot. One evening, after having dinner with him and his family, I got a *tuk-tuk* back to my lodgings and he provided me with a motor bike escort all the way home.

This vulnerable group had been omitted from the relief and recovery programme, and they became even more so after the disaster. The prison population experienced first-hand the devastating power of this natural phenomenon. They were also not allowed to attend funerals of loved ones on the outside. For some, when they were to be released, they would be going back to villages that no longer existed, or at least not in the way they left them after they were to be rebuilt.

With this in mind, I had to do something, however small. You may be asking yourself *Why a nursery and toilets?* For starters, I was aware of my limited resources and, at the end of the day, you can only do what you can do in that situation using what is available to you. More importantly though, it is an issue of well-being. I believe the protection of children is always of paramount importance; therefore, reducing risks that may cause a child significant harm must be addressed. The vulnerability of children is recognised widely within disaster studies and practice. When we as workers tackle issues of the vulnerability of children we are to balance these with the rights of the child as well as their welfare. Personally, in a disaster context, I would argue that children are the most vulnerable of the vulnerable.

After I returned to the UK, I received a phone call from the chief. He wanted to know how to spell my name so he could invite me back for a grand official opening of the nursery and toilet block I had built. Not my scene at all. I told him, "No, if you are going to have a plaque on the wall and an opening ceremony with important people and the press present, then you must write: 'This is a gift from the people of Wales and the Christians of Galle. You are to invite, on my behalf, the pastor of my church; he will represent me and the local community.'" So that is what happened. The words are carved in three languages—English, Sinhala, and Tamil—and you will find that plaque cemented on that wall to this day. So, if you find yourself in a sticky situation and locked up in Galle Prison, tell them you are from Wales; it might help, or maybe not!

During that post-tsunami time, I was married with a five-year-old child. Once I considered it to be safe, and the dead bodies had been dealt with, I made the decision to bring my daughter Blaze out to join me. We were out there as a family. In the morning, Blaze went to "jungle school," and in the afternoon I gave her the choice of playing with other children in our neighbourhood or coming to work with me.

During the time Blaze accompanied me in the afternoons, she got involved in distributing aid in the form of food, essential supplies, and new toys for the children. One afternoon she sang in front of a group of women and children in an internally displaced persons (IDP) camp.

Before we left the UK, the head teacher from a primary school got in contact with me. The children had donated their pocket money and placed the money in envelopes on which they had drawn messages of love and hope. I was invited to go and lead an assembly, and they donated their money through me, to go to help those affected by the tsunami. It was a special situation; I had the pocket money of Welsh children in my care, and I wanted to find a fitting cause to donate to. I came across a primary school in that community that had been affected directly by the tsunami. I was told that many of the children had lost everything, as their homes and belongings were totally destroyed by the great wave. I asked the principal of that school what he thought the children needed. He replied, "Shoes." So I took Blaze to a shoe shop, DSI, which is Sri Lanka's equivalent to Clarke's. I asked Blaze to choose one white school shoe for the girls and one black shoe for the boys. I then asked to speak with the manager of the shoe shop. I asked him if he had a lorry. He did. I told him I have five hundred children that needed new shoes and I did not know their sizes. I asked if he could load up a lorry with shoes, after showing him the two pairs Blaze had chosen. We arranged a date. The lorry arrived at the school early in the morning. Out jumped half a dozen men in uniform from the shoe shop, and boxes were unloaded into an empty classroom. We spent the day there. Class by class, children came to have their feet measured and were given a pair of shoes. Blaze assisted the men in unloading the lorry and handing the shoes to the children. When it came to break time, Blaze went out to the playground and ran around with the children. When we came home to the UK, I went back to the primary school that had donated their pocket money and did another assembly to tell them where their money had gone and showed them some photos. Blaze came with me, and I interviewed her about her experiences in front of the children in that school assembly that day.

This was not the first time Blaze travelled to Sri Lanka, nor the last. Other trips for her personal development followed. In the autumn of 2010, when she was eleven years old, I took her on a mission trip to Thailand with a group from the south coast of England. It was her trip, and I went as her chaperone. The purpose was to work with children and teenagers who had been rescued from child prostitution, and with children in a refugee camp on the northern border with Myanmar (formerly Burma). In the time we spent there, Blaze took part in telling stories through the medium of drama. Her other activities included singing, crafts, games, and simply hanging out with the other children. It was a good experience and education for her. For starters, before we went, I had to tell her about child prostitution which, appropriately, she thought was disgusting. Sometimes I wonder if I exposed her to too much, too young.

ROMANIA

In 1993, I married a wonderful, compassionate, sensitive, creative, funny man who loved me dearly and I him. He was a fellow member in the mission community where I lived, and he was a great companion to me. It was a large wedding with four hundred guests. My parents put on an amazing day full of surprises, including a guest appearance from Mickey and Minnie Mouse, a reception on the end of a pier with a Noddy train to get us down to the end, and the going-away vehicle was a Sunseeker yacht. Due to our lifestyle, which at that time did not include settling down and buying a house, we asked guests who were thinking of a customary present to instead give money for our next mission. With the wedding money, we bought a pickup truck and converted it into a safari jeep. We filled the jeep with half a dozen fifteen to sixteen year olds and drove across Europe to Romania that summer. The year earlier, we had gone out there to "reccy" the situation and stayed with members from the mission who lived out there. The purpose of this venture, along with the personal growth, development, and challenge for those travelling with us, was to work in an orphanage. We knew going into the orphanage would potentially be hard-hitting for the young people we took with us. The situation was just like what we'd seen on the television when Romania opened up to the West. There were a number of children in each cot, rocking back and forth, soaked in their own urine and vomit. The smell was strong to say the least. Yet they held their arms up and wanted to be picked up and hugged. As hard as it was, mainly due to the smell, how could you refuse to give a child warmth and affection? There were also teenagers in the orphanage the same ages as the ones we took on the trip. We set our young people to work, painting and decorating rooms in an attempt to brighten up the environment. Our time was also spent playing football in the grounds, which provided much fun and laughter for everyone. I know two young people we took on that trip who have gone on to do other missions of their own, one working in India. The spark ignited with us fanned into flame, a fire and passion for the world which spread into other nations.

UGANDA

Africa holds a special place in my heart. In my attempts to go there and give of the little I have, I have often found I end up receiving so much more. One particular trip to East Africa was personally transformative.

I went as part of a small team to encourage the local church. I was the only woman preacher. This was a role normally for the men, so I was the novelty card, so to speak. Personally, I don't mind that. Many people had not seen a woman standing up and preaching before. We had an itinerary of travelling around the country speaking at a number of churches. The other two preachers on the team were men who were pastors from traditional churches back in the UK. I was not a pastor, nor was I traditional, so I was initially worried. How could I perform in a manner that was in keeping with the others? I decided I couldn't, and I just needed to be myself. The church settings we visited were a mix of brick buildings completed, brick buildings not completed with holes for windows but no glass, a marquee, mud huts, bamboo huts, and even outdoors under a tree.

I was invited to speak. The reaction of the people was somewhat interesting. I was working with a translator which gave me time to think between each sentence. I found that common words were "Hallelujah" and "Amen," where no translation was required. The audience (congregation) did not sit there and quietly listen to what I had to say. Instead, people started shouting back in response. Then some started jumping up from the benches they were sitting on, raising their hands in the air, and making noises of celebration. In the middle of my talk, one chap who was at the back of the room ran down to the front and got on the drum and banged it repeatedly until I was finished.

As we travelled, word of this white woman preacher spread before we had even arrived. The space was not big enough for all. I could see people hanging through the windows, eyes peering through the bamboo slats. On one occasion, we were in a hut with a tin roof. The rain started; it got louder and louder. I began to shout my message so as to be heard, but it came to a point that the rain deafened me out. I shouted out, "Rain from heaven flooding this land with the blessings from God." At that point, the whole congregation jumped up, banged on the drums and sang and danced in the way only Africans can, until the rain stopped when I continued to finish off my preach.

During this trip, I was invited by one of the African pastors to speak at one of their "crusade" meetings. Basically, this was giving a talk to people in the community who were not church attenders. I went alone. First there was a talk about AIDS and giving out condoms. Then it came to the next stage of the public meeting. Drums started up, and people were singing and dancing. Now it was my turn to talk. What was asked of me was to give a "gospel message." I climbed the steps and stood on a swaying, rickety wooden platform. I looked out over the crowd; there were hundreds—thousands—of people gathered in the field. It was the biggest "gig" of my life! When I finished, a multitude ran up to the stage wanting to receive prayer and give their lives to Jesus.

I was given the nickname "White Fire." They said I preached like an African, but I was in a white body. I took this to be a great compliment. I know this, though: when I go to heaven, and we are all there worshipping God for the rest of eternity, I do hope I am surrounded by black Africans; but thinking about it, in coming face to face with the glory of God, I guess who you may be next to won't have any significance.

WEST AFRICA

In the autumn of 1987, we took our first overseas holiday to West Africa as a family. I was due to move into a life in the mission and my parents thought it would be a good idea for all the family to have a flavour of what mission life was like, hence travelling to West Africa to spend some time with the missionaries who lived there. We travelled by Aeroflot, the number-one airline of the Soviet Union. It was the cheapest way to get there and so that was our first mistake! The route was long: starting in London, then to Moscow, Russia, then to Budapest, Hungary, then to Tripoli, Libya, then to Bamako, Mali, then to Ouagadougou, Burkina Faso, and finally to Niamey, Niger. Not only was the route long but the Soviet airliner wasn't exactly known as being the best airline in the world. Caviar was served at 3 a.m., and the smell of bully beef turned my stomach. The air stewardesses weren't the most hospitable. We had to wait for hours for our connection in Moscow airport. At Budapest, we had to get out of the plane on the tarmac and walk through a line of soldiers with dogs on each side. At Tripoli, the ladies' toilets were ankle deep in water and urine, plus the local men stared at you. Of course, as if it wasn't enough to do it once, we had to endure it again on the route home. The homeward bound story is far more entertaining.

In Niger and Mali, we encountered the nomadic tribes people called the Tuareg, also known as the "blue people." They wore a turban and veil, and the indigo dye-coloured clothes stained their skin, hence the nickname. The Tuareg are predominantly Muslim. There are approximately two million of them living across the Sahara Desert. We were able to spend time with them in the desert and Sahel region, sitting and talking into the night by the glow of the fire. The Tuareg people have a popular tea called *atai* made from Gunpowder Green tea mixed with mint and sugar, poured three times in and out of the teapot, finally served by pouring into a small tea glass from a height which makes it froth. You have to have three cups of the stuff, otherwise it is considered to be rude. Furthermore, if they do not serve you three glasses, you better run, because you are in trouble! I struggled to drink it; it's certainly not my cup of tea, so to speak, but when you are in situations like that, you say the "missionary prayer," that being, "Lord, I'll put it down; you keep it down."

One afternoon, we were invited to a celebration of the birth of a child. Many Tuareg families had gathered. We sat and ate with them a dish served in a large bowl that was placed on the floor in the middle of a circle we sat in, and we all dipped into the food using our right hand. After the food, it was time for the music and singing to start. We were treated to a ceremonial sword dance which was performed by the men in a group, The Tuareg sword is called a *takoba*, and it's a fierce looking weapon which was waved around in the air during the dancing. The dancers were in full traditional costume, and it was a magnificent sight.

Going home, we travelled from Niamey back to Ouagadougou, where we were to spend some time with a black African pastor, his family and the church. Unknown to us at that time, a military coup was taking place in the capital, Ouagadougou, Burkina Faso. On the 15th October 1987 in a bloody battle, the president and twelve other officials were killed in a gun fight at the presidential palace. The president's body was riddled with bullets, and then dismembered. Fighting continued for several days and a curfew was imposed. We were travelling in an old Bedford army truck. Having crossed the border from Niger to Burkina Faso we decided to pull off the road early and camp in the bush. The next morning, in continuing our journey, we noticed an increase of army presence. We were stopped on the road at gunpoint and ordered out of the truck and lined up, while some of the soldiers pointed their rifles at us and others searched everything and threw items out onto the ground. Following this, we were allowed to get on our way and finish the journey. When we arrived in Ouagadougou, we learnt of the coup. It proved to be fortunate that we had pulled off the road the night before, as the timing of the execution of the coup and our riding in a military truck, mixed with the confusion among soldiers in the outposts at the time, could have caused difficulties.

We were due to fly back to the UK. However, all the borders had closed including flights coming into and going out of the country. Communications in and out of the country were also suspended. We were in lockdown. It was another two weeks before the first international planes landed and took off. A few days before we actually got on a flight home, we heard rumours that they were going to open the airport. We went down there to see what was happening. After being among the crowds of people wanting to leave and the resounding answer that what was happening was absolutely nothing, we were hungry and went on the search for food. On the way back to our lodging we found a road café. It was mid-afternoon, and the food had been warmed up in the pot for hours. Given the heat of the day and the time of day, this proved to be our second mistake! Yes, food poisoning. The worst food poisoning of our lives.

Eventually a plane from Aeroflot landed, and the time came when we were able to board for the multiple flights home. We were all so ill. However, when we arrived in Moscow, of course we had missed our connecting flight back to London by two weeks. Our passports were removed, and we were put on a bus and taken to a locked, guarded hotel where we spent three days. Alighting from the bus, we were marched the relatively short distance past Soviet military personnel restraining barking attack dogs lurching at us. On the second day in Moscow, though, I had a treat. The rest of my family were still too ill to get out of bed, but courtesy of the Russians, we got a bus tour of the sights of Moscow. We were not allowed out of the bus and the door was guarded by an armed soldier. Nevertheless, I had a good window seat, and we were given a tour guide who told us all about their version of Soviet history and of the buildings we saw. Mikhail Gorbachev was president, it was still the Cold War, *Glasnost* was very new ushering an era of "openness," and the fall of the USSR was in the future. As well as the beauty and colour of the buildings in Red Square, what struck me as we were driving through the streets was that there were not many cars on the road and people were queuing outside of shops. It was all very grey, in complete contrast to buildings on show like the Kremlin and St. Basil's Cathedral.

Finally, we all made it home to the UK and, as with all homecomings since that time, I had a ham sandwich to settle my tummy! On arriving home, we were to find ourselves as local celebrities, because for the past two weeks we had been featured in our local newspaper—first, as missing, then as being caught up in a military coup. The day after we came home, the newspaper wanted to interview us.

PLAYTIME

It wasn't all work. Alongside work, I always tried to have days of rest, if possible. Depending on the situation, with opportunities not always being appropriate, there were times when I was able to enjoy leisure activities that provided light relief.

Piranha fishing in Brazil is one highlight. Piranhas are indigenous to South America. I believe there are about thirty-nine different species of piranha, the red-bellied piranha being the ones with a reputation as the aggressive flesh eaters, dramatized in the 1978 movie *Piranha*, among other films. This depiction is somewhat of an exaggeration, but when you are there fishing in the Amazon for piranha, all that is in your head is "man eaters." One day a group of us spent a whole day piranha fishing from a small boat captained by a "crazy man." We were provided with a bamboo stick with an attached piece of string and a hook on the end. Rods were dangled over the side of the boat, and it wasn't long before someone had a bite. Everyone got extremely excited, with screams of joy. As each fish was pulled up from the water, others gathered around getting out their cameras to capture the moment. In the excitement, a camera was dropped into the water. The natural reaction was to try to catch the camera before it disappeared into the depths. As the owner's hand went into the water, everyone screamed in horror, shouting "Piranhas!" So, the captain got off the boat and gently sank into the water to look for the camera. People pleaded with him not to do it, to get back in the boat. But he disappeared under the water. A loud gasp was let out by all. Time seemed to stand still, all the passengers staring at the water in silence. And then, he surfaced. He was unable to find the camera and simply got back into the boat. Everyone could breathe again!

Once, when Blaze was six years old, I took her for a three-day excursion to a turtle sanctuary. We went to a United Nations-funded turtle conservation project. I don't know how I pulled it off, but the main man from the UN picked Blaze and me up in his 4x4 vehicle and drove us south to the project's base. It was the type of place where you take your own loo roll unless you want to use your hand! I remember this as being a special mother/daughter time. The first night we were there, we jumped in the 4x4 and were driven to the nearby beach, passing the incredible farting and rather stinky tortoise *en route*. The driver identified the tortoise immediately due to the smell, and then pulled over and located the offending creature. Blaze thought it was fantastic. When we arrived at the beach, a Green Turtle had come ashore and started to dig herself a hole in the sand to lay her eggs. Alongside a member from the project, Blaze helped to collect and count the eggs and put them in a bucket that we later re-planted in a safe zone in the sand, away from poachers. There were about one hundred eggs from that one turtle. During our visit, an older batch of eggs hatched, so we were involved in releasing the babies into the sea. On our second day we were joined for a few hours by a group of students from the UK. The main UN man gave a lecture on sea turtles. At the end of his talk, he opened up the floor for questions. The only hand in the air was Blaze's. Bear in mind, we were in a group of older students, and I was thinking *Oh no, what on earth is she going to ask?* Fortunately, it was actually an intelligent question about the length of time a turtle can remain underwater. After the talk had finished, Blaze went up to speak with the UN guy and asked him for a copy of his PowerPoint presentation, which he kindly gave her. Blaze took it home to show her friends and school teachers, telling them all about it. A proud Mummy moment!

Missions were many—travelling the globe, providing many a story to tell. They gave me a sense of purpose and made me feel alive.

Schizophrenia

The Wave

CHAPTER THREE
MADNESS

"You're mad, bonkers, completely off your head. But I'll tell you a secret.

All the best people are."

Alice in Wonderland

Elation

I HAVE A DIAGNOSIS OF schizoaffective disorder. So, what is that? What does that mean? How does it affect me? What are my symptoms? What has helped? What experiences have surprised me and what experiences have I learnt from?

SCHIZOAFFECTIVE DISORDER AND ME

Schizoaffective disorder is a combination of both schizophrenia and bipolar disorder. The idea that I could be mentally unwell felt totally unacceptable to me. For me, the issue of acceptance was the biggest hurdle to overcome. Once I was able to accept it, I was able to move forward, learning how to live with my diagnosis and symptoms in a way that allows me to press on in finding a level of stability whereby restrictions are limited, and I am able to enjoy life.

Initially it was believed that I had schizoaffective disorder depressive type, but it now appears I am actually of mixed type. Although any two people may have the same diagnosis, it may manifest itself in different forms for each of them. As each person is individual and unique, so too are the symptoms they experience and the way it affects their life. Having said that, there are also similarities which others with the same diagnosis can identify.

PSYCHOSIS AND ME

As I have already said, I am a voice hearer. My psychotic symptoms also cause me to see and feel things that others cannot. At the beginning of Chapter Two, I mentioned that in my left ear, I hear the voice of God. In my right ear, I hear the voices of "Tom" and "Jerry." Normally the voices of Tom and Jerry are quiet, like having a radio on in the background. However, there are also times when they get louder and louder, to the point that they are shouting at me. They can be nasty, they make demands, and they command. Tom's voice is murderous while Jerry's is suicidal. Jerry always wins over Tom. I have had times when I have felt someone lying on top of me. I can feel the weight and pressure on my body.

Around me to my right there is a girl with long blonde hair. She is dressed in a long white cotton nightshirt. She does not speak. She just stares at me, and she looks sad. To my left there is a man with his fist raised. In front of me, an old lady is laughing and cackling. Sometimes others come. It can become very loud when everyone starts shouting. I also experience demons coming through my bedroom door. I find this to be the most frightening of the things I see. I often get lifted, levitated horizontally, off my bed and spun around in mid-air by my ankles. On another occasion, many hands came through my mattress grabbing hold of me and trying to pull me through to the other side. I also see creatures. I see snakes and scorpions that are sometimes joined by rats and giant spiders. Most of the time they just run around the edges of the room, but there are also occasions when they come out into the room and attack me. One day a snake bit into my hand, and I couldn't shake it off. Their behaviour changes due to my status; when I am well, they are still there but not causing me any trouble, and the more unwell I become, the more active and vicious they are. So, I set traps for them.

As well as setting traps, I have responded to my sightings in a number of other ways. I have covered all the furniture in my lounge, including the TV and pictures on the walls, with white sheets. That means the creatures cannot hide and wait to jump out at me from behind the patterns on my furniture. I have made a "hedge of protection." I did this by writing Bible verses down on pieces of paper. I arranged the cards in a circle, and then I sat in the centre of the circle. Thus, the power in the words prevents the creatures from crossing the line and getting to me. These are a couple of examples, but there are more.

I have been told by others that during these times, I am quiet and do not speak for long periods of time. I find that interesting when they say that, because to me, there is so much conversation going on that I am a part of. The voices are continuous and so loud. For me, there is no quiet.

DEPRESSION AND ME

Depression can be crippling. My mood goes low, I don't want to do anything, and I think and feel bad about myself. It comes over me and I don't know where it has come from. I can't identify why it has gripped me in such a harsh way. It can last months and sometimes even years at a time. It is long-lasting. I cannot find enjoyment in anything, and I am unable to feel any form of pleasure. It is not something I can just snap out of, and only a fool would tell someone to do that. Depression first came over me in my early teens and has remained with me on and off throughout my life. It's not that I feel sad; I feel overwhelmed, worthless, critical and negative about myself. I have trouble sleeping even when I feel tired. There are other times when I sleep a lot. There have also been times when I have woken up in strange and unusual places and I don't know how I got there. I lose interest in eating. My concentration diminishes and my thoughts and actions slow down. I feel my life is pointless. When I am severely depressed, psychotic symptoms occur that I find disturbing, and they build up and become more distressing over time. I isolate myself from other people, and I go quiet. My daily routines are affected; I don't shower, and my personal hygiene and appearance is neglected. I stop doing my weekly food shopping and don't eat proper meals. Housework gets missed and I don't open my post.

MANIA AND ME

I didn't realise I had manic episodes, but I did know I have "very good times." I thought these times were what I should be like all the time, and I wanted to be able to live at that energy level. One day I was talking to a mother who was expressing concern that her daughter might be heading towards a manic episode. She was listing symptoms she felt were consistent with this being the case. In her list she said that her daughter had recently bought five DVDs. When I reflected on this conversation, I thought to myself, "If five DVDs indicate possible signs of forthcoming mania, and I've just bought twenty-one hats in the past three weeks, what does that mean?" It caused me to look afresh over my life, my actions, my thinking. I wrote down some thoughts on cards. I identified uncontrollable excessive spending; I seem to buy multiple items of the same thing. Along with numerous hats which are on the wacky side, I have thirty-eight watches, many of them not cheap. When I get something in my head, I can't stop thinking about it and

I have to do it—right now. My mind races and, at times, I find it hard to grab hold of my thoughts as they whiz around. I get easily frustrated and irritable. I become more talkative and jump from one topic to another. I am restless; I can't sit still. I get up in the middle of the night and move furniture around or start a project. One time I dug a hole in the garden and chopped a canoe in half and planted it in the hole, and on another occasion, I built a treehouse on top of the garage. I have bursts of high physical energy, lots of energy. I feel I can do anything; I feel indestructible. I like having a close shave with death, because it gives me such a rush. I have had the Arabic letter "N" tattooed on the back of my neck, just in case ISIS chops my head off, so they know they have got the right person, a Christian. In fact, I have gone further, and I have the whole gospel tattooed on my back and within a full sleeve, making my body a message.

RELAPSE SIGNATURES, RELAPSE PREVENTION, AND RELAPSE DRILL

In working with others, I have come to understand what takes place and what it looks like when I am starting to become unwell. These indicators are called "relapse signatures." In the symptoms, I have described how psychosis, depression, and mania affects me; these relapse signatures can be observed. In all three areas, I lose time and become very forgetful. I am told of conversations I have had, things I have done, places I have been, but I have no memory of these things. I also become suspicious of people, especially health care workers. I have heightened anxiety, and my stress levels rise.

Once I identified these signs and symptoms, I learnt to work out a plan of how to respond to them, insofar as things that I could do to help myself, and to know when it is time to get help from others. Learning ways to help myself was important to me in that it gave me strategies whereby I was taking charge and taking back the control over myself. Coping strategies and distraction techniques work for me in a way that gives me insight into my own triggers and how I can handle them. When the voices start to become louder, I talk back to them. I try to be creative by painting and playing my ukulele or mandolin. I listen to my vinyls or my music on other forms of media. I like to kayak, bodyboard, stand-up paddleboard (SUP), and go camping in my VW van. I try to continue with my weekly routines. I go and have meals with friends and spend time in the company of others. I am aware of when I need to be with friends and, with their help, identify when I need to seek professional assistance. Having a plan in place has been important, and it provides a safety net.

FRAMING OF QUESTIONS

Particularly in the early days of my diagnosis when I was struggling with the issue of acceptance, the way a question was asked of me was quite important. If I was asked the question "Are you taking your medication?" the answer was most likely "Yes." However, if asked the question "Are you taking your medication as prescribed?" then my answer may have been "No." Another question may have been "Have you harmed yourself?" The answer is "No." In reframing the question to "Have they (the voices) harmed you?" the answer could be "Yes." Equally, to the question, "Do you have any suicidal plans or intentions?" the answer would be "No." But by changing the question to "Do they have any plans to kill you or have they tried to kill you?" the answer could be a "Yes."

The way I look at it, I have never self-harmed or tried to commit suicide. When I am being burnt, my mind and my will do not want this. Physically I try to pull the hot poker away, but I am unable to do so until it goes cold. I feel it is beyond my power and control. I am not doing this to myself. I believe it is possible that one day they will get me. They will kill me. This is my fear.

MEDICATIONS

I have tried a few different medications. In general, there are two things I dislike about taking my pills:

1) They make me fat.

2) They suppress my creativity.

ANTI-PSYCHOTICS

Risperidone. Gave me high prolactin levels and I had no sex drive.

Aripiprazole. Gave me "the beans." I was restless. I couldn't sit down. I became physically uncomfortable not knowing what to do with myself. I couldn't sleep. I wore myself out. I had to stop taking them.

Quetiapine. My favourite, for its sedative affect.

MOOD STABILIZERS

Depakote (Sodium Valproate). Gave me the munchies. I was hungry all the time. I put on more weight.

Lithium. I could not try that one as it does not mix with the high blood pressure tablets I take. I would need to be closely monitored if I took lithium, so this wasn't a good option for me.

Other side effects of the medications, especially the anti-psychotics, are the links they have to chronic diseases, those for me being high cholesterol and diabetes. If you are on anti-psychotic medication for a length of time, as in years, there is a high likelihood you will develop other chronic diseases and thus end up on more medication.

Do they work? The quick answer is, yes, I believe they do. With regards to the anti-psychotic medication, I have found that they do not totally take away the psychosis, but the voices are muted to the point where I am not disturbed by them, and the visions are less frequent. I have found the antidepressant medication does lift my mood, but I have continued to be depressed even when taking the highest dose recommended. The mood stabilizer does not prevent ups and downs, but it does keep me in a band, so I don't go too high or too low. The trick, so to speak, with medication, is to take it consistently as prescribed. You cannot dip in and out. I have learnt it is not good when I take matters into my own hands and make my own decisions on when and how much medication I take. The key is to take the medication as prescribed by the psychiatrist. There are times when, under the supervision of the psychiatrist, the medication is either changed or tweaked. Sometimes the dose is increased and other times it is reduced. Equally, there have been times when, for one reason or another, a different medication may be required.

When it comes to medication, I believe it is a case of "pick your poison" and "suck it and see." Each person reacts differently to the same tablets. Just because I prefer *Quetiapine*, doesn't mean the next person would be able to tolerate it. Sometimes I struggle with the thought of taking medication, but I guess the fear of becoming seriously unwell again outweighs everything else. I want to be slimmer, more active, more daring, take more risks, feel the adrenalin, be more creative, achieve more than I do. Stability is a challenge for me; it feels like a dirty word. However, there is a "but." The trade-off. I am a medicated version of myself. I miss what I would consider to be the good times of the old Laura. I have become one person and I want to be another person. I have had to consider the price—make a shift in my outlook—and look at what is more important. From there, I make my decisions and choices.

THERAPY

I think the best advice from a therapy session—in the form of a distraction technique, doing something that will take your mind off the way you are feeling—was to "Chew on a chilli!" Personally, I can't think of anything more ridiculous, but I can imagine that, should you give it a go, it would definitely distract you. I have had ideas of designing and creating my own "Chew on a Chilli" brand of T-shirts, featuring "Schizo Chilli," "Psycho Chilli," "Manic Chilli," "Depressed Chilli," and so forth. I didn't think it would be particularly PC, though!

Medication alone is not the only form of treatment in moving towards a recovery phase of your illness. Talking therapies can be helpful, as can a psychosocial approach. Some people also draw upon the strength that can be found in their faith and spirituality. A holistic approach led by the individual themselves is, I believe, important in sustaining recovery.

I rate CBT (cognitive behavioural therapy) for psychosis. This is not standard CBT. Instead, it focuses directly on the psychosis. The aims are to reduce the distress and fears caused by the voices, visions, and other forms of psychotic experiences, and to improve your quality of life by teaching you to manage stress and anxiety. It tackles your thoughts, feelings, and actions. In doing so, it brings you back in touch with reality. I had a good therapist, and I went to sessions weekly for some months. Homework was given. One piece of homework for me was to research scorpions in the UK. The purpose of this was to cause me to question whether what I was seeing in my living room was really there. It helped my mind to shift, to look at things from a different angle and perspective. Together we worked out my relapse signatures, warning signs, and personal coping strategies. These remain important as an aid to assist me and those close to me to recognise and act, should the need arise.

WORK

Understandably, I have had time off from work when I have been unwell. My career in the child and family department of social services did not come to an end as I would have liked. I loved my first five years in child protection. I was doing really well in my role, and I was promoted into a senior post. When I became unwell, and after being admitted to periods on the psychiatric ward, I moved on from being a frontline worker and took up a role in leading a team that provided support to families directly working with young people and their parents in trying to keep them together. It was a supportive service that frontline social workers could refer to for time-limited pieces of work, to aid the assessment process and often to address teenage issues that were causing difficulties within the family unit. I did not ask for a change in role, nor was I interviewed for the job alongside other candidates, because the job was not even advertised. The post just appeared one day with my name on it. There were aspects of the job I liked, but the role really wasn't me. It was office-based, there was no interaction with clients, and it was a management role which, I might add, I did as a senior social worker, not a manager. There were a lot of duties that I personally found soul-destroying—form filling, collecting data and statistics, dealing with issues of staff, and rotas held no interest to me.

Due to the latest departmental restructure, of which in my time there were many, my role changed again. I was slipped into another role that was again of no interest to me. But then, a job is a job, right? No, not for me. I need to enjoy what I do, have a sense of calling. If I don't, I struggle in my mental health. I take my hat off to people who do jobs that, for them, are just jobs, and they keep doing them year in, year out. I don't have the strength of character to do that. One day I was called to a meeting where I was strongly encouraged—by management, my union representative, and the HR nurse—to take some time out. I agreed I wasn't very well. My mood was low, I struggled to concentrate, and I was distracted, so my ability to effectively lead the team I managed was beginning to suffer. I went on sick leave, and a few months later, my GP signed me back in as fit to work. However, management did not want me to return to work. Numerous meetings took place, and I was ordered to see the occupational health doctor. In total, I saw eight doctors over a two-year period, one of which was my own psychiatrist who provided a report. All eight doctors declared me fit to work. Even after each report was submitted to management by doctor after doctor, each stating I was fit to return to work, management would not accept or agree with their findings. They would not allow me to return to work, and I remained at home. Because my GP was no longer providing sick notes, I was put on what they call "garden leave." I was at home for two years on full pay. There came a point when my managers stopped attending meetings and it was left with just me, my union representative, and the HR officer. Which managers were behind the HR officer, I do not know. Although I did not always like the message that my HR officer brought, I did appreciate her straight talking, and she was very good at responding to my emails.

There were a few twists and turns, but in the end I was given the opportunity to have a trial period as a social worker in the community mental health team. I was excited to be given the opportunity. I would be back working with people, outside the office, no staffing responsibilities, able to get on and be responsible for my own work. It was a privilege and a big deal for me to be working with clients who, like me, have severe and enduring mental health conditions—some of them with the same diagnosis as mine. The initial agreement was for me to have a one-month trial, at the end of which, management would make a decision whether I would be offered a full-time post there or not. I was provided with an excellent induction. Another meeting was called, and the one-month trial turned into two months. I actually agreed that this was a good idea, given that most of the time during the first month was going around visiting venues connected to the service. I needed more time to work directly with my clients. In working in that team, I decided that it would be important that, from the beginning, I was open and honest with management about my own mental health, so as to protect myself and the service. I compiled a booklet on my diagnosis, relapse signatures, early warning signs, relapse prevention, and drill including names of relevant people and the role they have in my life. This was passed up to senior management. Someone up top freaked! I was called to another meeting and was offered a different job. It was also said that I would need to see another doctor. I couldn't believe it. For the first time in two years over this issue of work, I cried. I politely declined the offer of the other job and questioned why I needed to see another doctor when I had seen eight already. I was able to continue my trial period. Following further meetings, it was actually another four months before I was appointed in post. In my final meeting with my HR officer, which was for the purpose of officially telling me I was to be appointed in the post, it turned out to be just her and me present as no one else was able to make the meeting. Given we had worked together for over two years, I was pleased to be able to speak with her personally, because the journey had been—to say the least—an interesting one. I appreciated her final words to me: "I can't fault your tenacity."

But that is not the end of the story. During the trial period, we had put in place support for me in the form of personal supervision with a senior social worker, which was separate from my manager's supervision on my cases. I welcomed this, and it was good to touch base with someone on a personal level. After I was given a full-time post in the team, I think I got a bit over-excited which led to a small manic episode. My daughter was the first to recognise it, but I also noticed things like the twenty-one hats I had bought online over a couple of weeks. I shared with my senior my thought cards, which questioned and identified possible signs that I may be experiencing mania. She shared this with the manager who invited me into his office and said he wanted me to take a few weeks off. I saw my psychiatrist and discussed the matter. I was taken off the anti-depressant medication and later prescribed a mood stabiliser. I was off work for three weeks after which I was able to return. However, senior management saw my thought cards that had questioned these possible manic episodes. This wasn't in my original booklet and was new information. There were twenty-two cards with a variety of potential indicators and symptoms listed, some of which were historic. The ones picked up were the ones that had written on them "machete," "hunting knife," and "bulletproof vest." The next thing I knew, the police turned up on my doorstep wanting to see my so-called weapons. They asked me why I had them, and they were interested in the bulletproof vest as well. I satisfied them with my responses, and they left. My senior phoned me the next day having heard that I had had "visitors." She expressed that both she and the manager were horrified and were sorry this had taken place as that was not an action they would have taken. I admit I was angry that someone had called the police on me. My response was to buy an axe, because after all, aren't all schizophrenics mad axe murderers? WRONG! Despite my initial reaction. I still thought that an open and honest approach was the way forward, and I have not held back in sharing personal information. Although I don't know who took this action, I forgive them, as I believe it showed their lack of knowledge and understanding about mental health more than anything else.

HEARING VOICES SUPPORT GROUP

I thought about going to a hearing voices support group. I had never been to any form of group therapy and had not met with others who have experiences similar to mine, other than when I was in hospital. On the internet I found a group in another town, not the one where I live and worked. It was an evening group, so I could go after work. I wanted to meet others who were voice hearers. I wanted to be able to discuss psychosis and how it affects me. I wanted to listen to and learn from other people's experiences in that area. I wanted to meet other professionals who hold down full-time demanding jobs and see how they manage and cope in balancing their mental health with their occupations.

The group was not as I had hoped it would be. Again, I was in a situation where I was the odd one out; I was the only person who went to work. For the most part, people just talked about their daily lives, and there was very little conversation about living with psychosis. I did try to initiate conversation in that area on a few occasions, but it was limited. The facilitator of the group did, however, provide me with a couple of handouts from the Hearing Voices Network which were of interest to me. When I drove the forty-five-minute drive home after the meetings, I often wondered why I had gone, but I also hoped that the next meeting would be different. Unfortunately, it wasn't. I did share with them what my job was, and I think they were somewhat surprised and taken aback by that information.

Come and Go

She Wants to be Amongst the Stars by Blaze

CHAPTER FOUR
MY CRAZY MOTHER, MY CRAZY FRIEND

"A true friend is someone who thinks you are a good egg even though he knows you are slightly cracked."

Bernard Meltzer

Laughing Water

FAMILY

FOR THOSE CLOSE TO A person with a mental health condition, life can be somewhat of a roller coaster. The ups and downs of both joy and pain impact on our relationships and shared experiences.

A DAUGHTER'S STORY

Life with my mum when I was very young was how I imagine every child felt towards their family; you look at both your parents with the notion that they're perfect and don't do wrong. For a long while, my mum was just my mum—except nothing like other mums. But it wasn't like I was any other child either. Mum and I are both known for being different.

The adventures my mum took me on were the highlights of my early life. Without exposure to different cultures, I don't think I would be the person I am today.

Exploring Sri Lanka multiple times, going to Thailand, and doing charity work in both places exposed me to inequalities as well as lifestyles that most children have never and will never experience.

A therapist once asked me if I felt that being exposed to disaster and very upsetting scenes negatively affected me, especially as I was so young. I think, because I was so young, I never understood the gravity of those situations at the time. If another child needed shoes, I gave them shoes. If another child needed toys, I gave them toys. My experiences opened my mind in a way that I'm grateful for. I'm so glad for my mother in her un-medicated state—which was neither bad nor good from a child's eye. She took me on her dangerous adventures, but still managed to keep me safe. I could run, laugh, play, and perform with no worries, because she and the people she trusted around me made sure I was okay.

These experiences have even made me decide that whenever I have a family, I want to show my children a life beyond their doorstep.

When I got to secondary school, I felt that my relationship with Mum changed. I was too young to understand why she was in and out of hospital, and when I eventually found out the answer was schizophrenia, I couldn't comprehend what such a diagnosis meant. Through online research, I could only understand she heard and saw things that no one else around her could hear and see.

As an only child with no cousins in the family, I had to express what was going on to my friends at the time—to which they replied that my mother was crazy and in a mental asylum. With so much love for her, I was very hurt to hear that was a friend's first thought. My own mother, crazy. When I look back at it now, that's when my dissociation towards my mother started. She wasn't this perfect role model; she was my crazy mum who kept secrets from me.

Going home to her became harder, and every time I entered the house there was something new, something "weird." Thoughts of a mental asylum appeared in my mind, and I then became terrified of what could happen to "my crazy mum." Research told me about suicide, self-harm, and other evil behaviour that was part of this condition, but it wasn't just schizophrenia now. It was schizoaffective disorder.

More and more, I'd see her mood change. One day she would be stuck in bed, then she would spend so much money on the strangest of things. My mind would flash to thoughts of her eventually hurting herself or committing suicide. The pain of these thoughts and the unpredictability of her condition made me need to separate myself from the whole situation, from my nan expecting me to look after her.

Since all this confusion surrounded me, I got severe depression, wanted to avoid going to school, and even began to self-harm. It was so difficult to love my mother, so difficult to associate myself to her— especially with all the negative comments from my father, too. My mind was stuck on how the world saw mental illness, and it was a trap I couldn't get out of for years. I couldn't look at my own mother as a regular person who has issues, like any other person, just like myself.

Finally, at age nineteen, I went on my own journey to Amsterdam for a year, and when I came back, I could finally look at my mum from a human perspective. She couldn't help having the personality traits that her illness gave her; she wasn't at fault for being unpredictable. Now I have so much admiration for her strength to suffer through everything and help those in need, to raise a daughter, to settle into demanding jobs so she could live. The main thing I admire about her is her ability to survive and cope through a time when her own daughter couldn't even hug her properly.

I wish I had been there for her more; I wish I could've understood the condition quicker. It hurts me so much that, because of something beyond her control, she received more pain of not having her daughter with her.

Part of me believes if there was less of a stigma around mental health, I wouldn't have wanted to separate myself as much—but there was still no stopping unpredictability.

We as humans tend to find comfort in the known and unchanged. What my very short life has taught me is to try to find comfort in the unknown, to ride the wave. I've ridden most of the wave with my mum's condition, and I have received the very best gift life could've given me: a closeness and love with my mum that I struggled to even imagine.

A MOTHER'S STORY

I tried to protect Blaze, my daughter, from my mental illness during her childhood. I didn't want her to become a child carer. Nevertheless, as I found out later, all she wanted to know was what was going on and why I kept going into hospital. When she was twelve years old, she moved out from my home and went to live with her dad. When Blaze turned eighteen, she became my "nearest relative" as defined under the Mental Health Act. She is acutely sensitive and aware, having amazing insight, and she knows when something is wrong even before I recognise it myself.

I never wanted to have children; it wasn't in my plan due to my lifestyle. I wanted to travel the world, and I believed having a child would be restrictive. I was also concerned that the lack of family stability—not just the travelling but also the imbalances in my mental health—would be detrimental to a child. After a few years of marriage, my position on this changed and I thought maybe one child would be manageable. One night I had a dream of a young child, a blonde-haired girl who called me "Mummy." At the same time, my husband had a dream that we had a child, seeing a dark-haired baby. The following year Blaze was born on my thirtieth birthday, and what a birthday present! She was a dark-haired baby and became a blonde-haired toddler and child. Blaze was very much wanted even before she was conceived. We wanted our little girl. When asked during a prenatal scan if we wanted to know the sex of our baby, I looked at the nurse and told her, "It's a girl." The nurse checked and confirmed it; we really were having a girl.

If you are wondering about her name, yes, it was me who named her, Blaze Tallulah. As you already know, I believe names to be important. "Blaze" represents fire, passion, a firebrand. "Tallulah" means laughing water, and it speaks of joy. Fire and water are two of the symbols that represent the Holy Spirit. I wanted my daughter to grow up not only knowing the presence of God but to become a person wildly devoted to the passion within her heart. I wanted her to one day stir up passions within others seeing change, truly radical and maybe even revolutionary. Equally, I wanted there to be the mark of laughter and joy upon her life, and I didn't want her to sink into the depression that I have known.

When Blaze was born, I can't say I felt an instant connection and bond with my baby. I made the decision that every time I picked her up from the crib, I would say, "I love you" out loud. The feelings began to flow. I tried and failed to breastfeed. While attempting to feed her one afternoon, I held her and cried. In my tears, I said to her, "I've let you down already. I'm so sorry," and that was in the first week of motherhood. I felt such a failure. About two weeks after the birth, I went back on anti-depressant medication, after having stopped them while I was pregnant. During the months and years ahead, I had help in caring for her. My husband played a role, joining in with feeds including the night time ones. We also had Blaze's godmother who often took her out and even had her overnight from a very young age.

Having a child caused me to establish routines. It made me get out of bed in the mornings, to have set meal times, and to shift my focus and care for a little person that I was responsible for. Having a child kept me going.

I made the mistake of thinking Blaze would enjoy the things I did. I took her swimming, to the beach, and camping—and to a point, she did enjoy it. But it became clear she was not a sporty person and her interests and gifts lay elsewhere. We went out and about in child-friendly settings and I met up with other mums with small children.

The greatest and most longstanding friendship that I made was with a family with whom I remain the closest of friends to this day. The mother was on her fourth child, that being the one Blaze had a friendship with, and later with child number five, too. This friend of mine went on to have eight children, and she has home-schooled all of them. She is an amazing woman and mother. We have a few things in common: we were both in the mission, although not at the same time as each other, and we both enjoy the great outdoors. Water sports, a beach life, and camping are our shared interests, along with our faith. She has been there through the rough and the smooth. When I was unwell, they had me over for meals on a weekly basis and, when things were particularly tough, daily. When it was not safe for me to be alone at night in my own home, I have slept at theirs. They have provided so much support and care for me over the years. My friend has always believed in me, not accepting the symptoms of my illness as being what defines me as a person.

Ultimately, the instability of my mental health drove Blaze away. She was struggling to live with me and wanted to be with her dad. I was also aware he wanted her with him. There was no custody battle; I didn't fight to keep her. I didn't believe a war between her parents would be good for Blaze, and I knew her dad is great with young people and would be a fantastic father, giving her all she needed at this stage of her life. I knew she was in the best place. The risk of this move, however, would be that his negativity towards me might influence her thoughts towards me, but that was a risk I had to take.

During Blaze's teenage years, I was predominantly the "taxi service," because her dad does not drive. I saw her on a weekly basis by taking her to drama school and singing lessons. When she got in the car, she would put her music on and sing at the top of her lungs for the entire journey, and sometimes she talked non-stop. I just listened. When she got out of the car, I leaned in to give her a kiss on the cheek and said, "I love you." I downloaded some of her music to my iPod and I played it when she was not with me, when I was missing her. Sometimes I would take her in my VW T25 van which both she and her friends loved. When she was younger, I would switch on the "Dukes of Hazzard" horn as I came round the corner to her drama school. With her friends, she would run up, and they all jumped in the back, sitting there talking and laughing together. She asked me to take her and her date to the school prom in my T25. I've held on to these moments, which, though small, are extremely precious to me.

I kept her bedroom as her room, just as she left it, but she never came to stay over. As she got older, I decorated it and I changed it to have a double bed for when she got a serious boyfriend. I wanted to provide somewhere that they could go. She has always had a key to the house if she'd wanted to come round, but her room remained unused. I would tell myself, *it is because she is a teenager and teenagers like to lead their own lives and don't really want their parents around.* But in my heart, I felt that my mental health was still the problem. We did spend time together at Christmas and on our birthday. In fact, we always saw each other on our birthday.

On Blaze's sixteenth birthday, I took her on a trip for a month. We went to Japan and Sri Lanka. For a long time, Blaze had wanted to go to Japan. She was at one stage very much into manga, a form of Japanese cartoon art. We spent two weeks in Tokyo. Japan held little appeal for me, but I wanted to take the opportunity to do something with her that she desired to do. I used the opportunity to test out her ability to travel, because it might not be long before she set out on her own travels exploring the world. I wanted to see if she could get from point A to point B in an unknown place, and if she could do it safely. We made a plan of daily activities and places to visit for the duration of our stay. There were days when I put Blaze in charge of planning the route, getting us to where we wanted to go and making sure we were fed and watered along the way. One day she did this with the assistance of Google, following her phone as people of her generation do. The following day, I asked her to put her phone in her pocket and said, "Today we are going old school! Here is a map." I told her, "Phones are great, but what do you do if you lose charge and the battery runs out?" She did great. We travelled on all different forms of transport, she read the signs, followed the directions, and successfully got us to places. And a great plus was, we didn't get lost. She also had an ability to communicate with local people, asking for assistance or giving instructions when in a taxi, being friendly. I knew she was ready, and it gave me great peace of mind.

About a fortnight after Blaze had her nineteenth birthday, at the beginning of August, she informed me, "Mum, I am going to live and work in Amsterdam." My response was, "Great, crack on, lovely." I didn't give her any help. Online, Blaze found herself a job and place to stay, and on August bank holiday weekend I took her to the airport. I did go out and visit her a couple of times while she was there. Although I was proud of her and proud of the independent woman she was becoming, I felt further separation and loss as I was not really part of her new life. A year later, she returned to the UK. When she came back, we got talking and I offered for her to come and live with me. She said she wanted to give it a go. I couldn't believe it! She hadn't lived with me in eight years, so I never imagined or thought this would ever happen. With Blaze coming home after all these years, it also gave me a level of anxiety. I didn't even know what food my own daughter liked to eat. Surely a mother should know these basic things about her own child. Ever since her return from Amsterdam, it has been a time of restoration and healing for both of us. I am so thankful, and I am loving the time I am able to spend with her. The nature of our relationship has changed again as we relate to one another, adult to adult, woman to woman, while still being mother and daughter. It has grown into a friendship. She has grown into a beautiful woman.

For the large part, I feel I missed my daughter's teenage years. There was a physical and emotional distance. I felt a great sadness, immense guilt, and like I was a rubbish mother. I caused my daughter pain and suffering. But now, that which was destroyed by mental illness is being renewed by grace and love in ways I never thought possible.

A WIFE'S STORY

I was married for fourteen years. Our first home was a tent pitched on Gower for the first six months of our new life together. At the beginning, we had fun times as we worked, travelled, and played together. Before we got married, my fiancé was aware of the ups and downs of my mental health. He thought it wouldn't be problematic and expected he would cope well with it. However, when I was unwell, he struggled more and more. There came a stage where he didn't want to come home; he dreaded the thought of it. He didn't know what he was going to walk into, how he would find me, and it proved to be too much for him. Even with the help of others, he couldn't cope. It would be good at this point for him to tell you his story in living with me, but unfortunately, that is not possible. As I have already mentioned, one of the things about being unwell is losing time, and so I have huge gaps in my memory; I can't recall events. What I do know is—initially—it was good. We loved each other very much. We were married for six years before Blaze came along. Due to the nature of our lifestyle, we were with each other all the time. We had many shared experiences.

We found ourselves in Reading, England, for a few months. Four years before our marriage finally came to an end, I knew I had lost my husband. I lay there in bed one night next to him and cried all night because he was no longer with me emotionally. His attitude and behaviour towards me had already started to change, and when we returned to our house in Wales this became more noticeable. I tried to make things right by doing things for him, but I guess this was not what he was looking for. The damage had already been done and I was unable to patch things up regardless of my efforts. I thought going to Sri Lanka post-tsunami would be just what we needed to bring us back together, but it was not. After we returned to the UK, at some stage he moved out of our bedroom into the front room downstairs. He was at this point working as a postman. When he came home from work, he played games on his Xbox or whatever device it was. I cooked for him, presenting him with meals, and I did the washing and cleaning. I got nothing back; he couldn't even hold a conversation with me. He announced he wanted to leave me and get a divorce. It was another year before he actually left. I do confess it wasn't easy living under the same roof at this time. I had mixed feelings. Right up until the time he left, I hoped he would change his mind and our marriage could be restored. However, I also got frustrated as it was becoming more and more difficult. I was doing my masters dissertation. He wasn't happy for me to work on it until after Blaze had gone to bed each evening. I wrote my dissertation in the shed by candlelight as it was the only way I could go about it. My frustration at this point boiled over, and after he went to work one morning, I knocked down the wall between the front and rear living rooms so he no longer had his own room. When he came home and saw what I had done, I said, "Ta da, we've often talked about knocking through to have a larger lounge." He didn't say anything. What's more, it didn't appear to have the desired effect. He only moved out after he'd gone to court to get the divorce and the judge turned him away telling him to come back when he had actually left the family home.

When I got married, I believed it was for life. My mental health destroyed our marriage. He left. I feel so sorry to him for everything he went through with me and the way it affected his life. His ultimate response towards me was that my mental health brought out the worst in him. When he left, he was not the man I married; I had zapped the fun, laughter, and life out of him. I have never bad-mouthed him to Blaze, nor have I allowed others to do so, even when it was clear Blaze was hearing things from her dad that were negative about me. He is her dad, a great father, and unfortunately, I am no longer able to call him "husband" or "friend." When I was in hospital, it was him I wanted to comfort me. When I think about him, the pain I caused him, the loss and separation, it causes me to well up with tears. There is a part of me that misses him, and to a degree, I still love him, but, just as he has, I have moved on. I have found new life and love in an unexpected place.

BARBARA'S STORY—COLLEAGUE AND FRIEND

Laura Ruth and I have known each other since January 2009. We were both working in a busy front-line Child Protection Team in Social Services. In June 2020, while we were all getting more accustomed to the new life under COVID lockdown restrictions, Laura told me that she was writing a book, and she asked if I would contribute to it. At first, I felt honoured, but also quite nervous about not being able to live up to the expectations. Sitting down and starting the process of writing down my thoughts was not easy. We all know that friendships have their ups and downs, but I feel that my friendship with Laura has been a personal challenge at times. It has taught me a lot about myself—my lack of understanding, my impatience, and how I crumbled under pressure. It also taught me how our society is running on the expectation of people having to fit in, and if they don't fit, they can get lost in the process. I am glad that Laura and I made it and that we are still friends today. I am grateful for Laura "letting me in" and the time we spend together.

As I said above, Laura and I met in early 2009 in a busy child protection team working for a local authority. Work was busy and demanding and the local authority was working under special measures, not being able to meet its statutory duties. I had started in the spring the year before, and by the time Laura and I met, our teams were merged. I was reserved and unsure about our teams merging, as my old team was split up in the process and most people went to a different team. Laura was one of the new team members who stood out from the start. She was loud, chatty, and always up to mischief. At random times in the day, mostly when stress levels were at their highest, she would get her harmonica out and play a song. I used to joke with Laura about her musical abilities, saying that although she was enthusiastic, she was not necessarily talented! Most of Laura's actions led to laughter and released some of the stress. Not everyone in the team appreciated this at the time!

There was an occasion where we had a team-building day. Laura took it upon herself to organise a treasure hunt. Now, Laura was known for talking in riddles at the best of times, so her cryptic clues that sent us around the locality were somewhat of a challenge. To stand any chance of getting round the course, we first had to get into the head of Laura. It was, however, great fun, even though a bit of a wild goose chase, and we probably used more petrol than necessary as we bombed around in our cars trying to beat the other teams to the finish line.

I always observed Laura to thrive on high stress levels and pressure. She told me stories of her past life, and despite our different political and religious beliefs, I always admired her for her passion and work with vulnerable communities at times of crisis. Social work is emotionally demanding, and managing risk is an anxiety-provoking exercise, but when I think back, I always felt that Laura had everything under control and tons and tons of resilience. When I am stressed, I get tense, and my responses to other people can be abrupt. Laura was always the one who picked up on this and cracked a joke, so I would be able to calm down and continue.

We worked closely together for about ten months before our employer had to make changes to the structure of the department once again. This was the end of Laura and me, and we were put in different teams. Laura and I had already started to be friendly outside of work; for example, we went together to see her lovely daughter in a theatre production.

I thought that Laura and I would carry on as we did before, have a laugh together in the office and see each other outside of work occasionally. But with her move to a different team, Laura and I lost touch. It started off with Laura not being around in work. I knew that Laura needed an operation back then, and I thought that she finally had an appointment for this. Some weeks later, I still had not seen Laura back in the office. I approached her manager and asked if everything was okay with Laura. Her manager told me that she was not allowed to talk about it.

Laura returned to work at one point, but she was off again shortly afterward. She then moved from that team, and then she moved yet again. Laura and I had some contact in between but I did not recognize Laura anymore. The fun-loving, carefree, and witty Laura had gone. The new Laura I met was more subdued and slower in her thinking.

Laura and I are both lovers of the outdoors and camping. Some core members of our old team got together for drinks in a pub. It turned out that Laura and I had each bought a T25 VW campervan, and our love for the outdoors and the vans brought us back together. So we moved on to being seasonal friends going for the odd camping trip together.

A couple of months later, work brought us back together. I took up a position in the Family Support Service where I was working alongside Laura. I would say that this was the most difficult time in our friendship. Family Support brought challenges that were different from those in front line child protection. Unfortunately, there was a culture of bullying, that is, not being allowed to openly discuss issues, as well as the constant threat of job cuts needing to be made. Surviving in a work environment is tough, and I could see Laura becoming unwell. Laura confided in me, telling me that she had a diagnosis of mental health difficulties, despite our employer requesting that she not share this fact with her work colleagues. Initially, I was trying to support Laura as best as I can, but I was out of my depth. Instead of speaking up and becoming a whistle-blower, I tried to keep the system running. I took on too much and it all fell apart, and Laura had to move to a different position again.

It hurt me to see Laura in such a dark and low place. The bubbly, funny person was gone, and sometimes, Laura would only say two or three sentences during the entire day in the office. I found this hard to manage, and I don't think I ever properly managed the situation. I desperately missed the bubbly, fun-loving, and strong friend I first came to know.

We lost touch a second time, but we were able to reconnect with more ease this time round. Now, we have moved on from being seasonal camping friends to enjoying each other's company regularly. We confide in each other, and I have learnt that we don't always have to chat, but can also sit in silence around the fire, enjoying the quiet times of life.

SUE'S STORY—FORMER MANAGER AND FRIEND

Laura Ruth came into my life in 2007. She was an agency social worker; I was the manager of a Social Services Child and Families Initial Assessment Team. I interviewed her for a vacancy and offered her a social work post. I very soon came to like her. I enjoyed her somewhat unusual ways and admired her for the adventures and missionary work she had previously been involved in. Her manager appreciated her resilience and her willingness (even enthusiasm) to happily go into any situation, and I found her to be a solid team player and generally a good person to have around.

We became friends; she made me laugh. Laura loved the buzz of the child protection visits and investigations, and we often chuckled at the tales of her visits. I probably shouldn't admit that, but it was such a stressful environment that when we were overwhelmed and snowed under with work, Laura was always calm and dependable. She formed strong relationships with colleagues in the team, the department, and with partner agencies. We joked with Laura about how she always carried a clipboard on visits and the fact that she kept her ID badge in a wallet and flashed it like a police warrant card. You couldn't not like Laura.

During this period, Laura developed a physical health condition, eventually sorted out with surgery, which was quite debilitating. We often suggested she take some time off work when it was causing her problems, but she insisted on carrying on. She was quite weak at times but that didn't deter her. One day she went out on an initial visit, and before she had reported in or come back to the office, I had a phone call of a complaint from the grandmother she'd visited; the social worker who had just visited her was clearly drunk! To my knowledge, Laura never touches alcohol, so it didn't seem likely. But her subsequent explanation of the circumstances of the visit was hilarious. This may not be completely accurate, but this is how I recall Laura describing the incident: this was the first visit to the family home on this particular case. Laura drove to the area, could see the house at the bottom of a bank from where she had stopped her car, but she couldn't find the road which would take her directly outside the property. She decided to make her way down the muddy bank (it had been raining) on foot to the street below. She slipped, and after falling on to her stomach, "surfed" down the bank on her clipboard, arriving face-down in the mud outside the front door of the home of the family she was visiting. She straightened herself up and checked it was the right door but, dishevelled and dirty, she didn't feel able to knock at the door and go in. Through the window, the grandmother saw Laura staggering around outside and falling over, and it didn't make the best impression on the grandmother. Laura was somehow able to walk up to the main street where she then collapsed and was found unconscious by two policemen. When Laura came to, she informed the police she was a social worker and showed them her ID badge. Laura heard them say, "Well, it looks real." A while later, I had a phone call. It was the police asking if I knew Laura Ruth. I was informed that Laura had been taken by ambulance (complete with flashing blue lights and sirens) to A&E.

Laura and I got on partly I think because she liked my straight talking. It is ironic that she describes herself in the book as a straight talker because most people who know her quite well have often been frustrated by her riddles and omissions. Many times I have said to her, "Laura, I'm a simple type of person. Will you please stop talking in riddles and just tell me what is on your mind?"

Being Laura's manager was not without its challenges; she had an unconventional dress sense, and it would also be fair to say that written work was not particularly her forte. I could tell that pulling together longer assessments, particularly those that had to be written in a prescribed style and format such as for court proceedings, didn't interest her, but she tried hard and would don her yellow-lensed dyslexia glasses and do her best to knuckle down. Even her short assessments were written a bit too colloquially, although you could say she was a forerunner inasmuch as social work (at least child and family work) is now all about simple language and avoiding jargon.

Those were the good times. Laura was entertaining, endearing, enjoying work, and getting on with the job as a single parent bringing up her daughter, Blaze, and enjoying her camping, camp fires, garden, family visits, and her chaplaincy at Asda. I knew that she missed being part of a church and was hurt about this. She did talk a bit about her struggles with her feelings, her beliefs around faith and worship, and the way she had been treated by members of her former church organisation, but it was years later that she talked about what had happened to cause this rift.

The first indication that something might be amiss or that Laura was a little more than an unusual "character" was when she said to me, "You know when you hear that other voice in your head?" I replied, "No, Laura what do you mean the other voice? Do you mean self-talk or talking to yourself?" "No," said Laura, "I mean, I really do hear a voice in my head." Soon afterward, it was clear that Laura was becoming mentally unwell, and I thought back to what she had said, and I felt that she had probably been testing me to see how I would take her revelation, how I would react, whether she could trust me. I may be completely wrong, of course. At that time, she also sent a few of her closer colleagues some very strange texts, often in the early hours. From what I can remember, they would have references to trees, flames, fire, and stars. The following day, she wouldn't remember she had sent them.

I can't really remember how things progressed from there to what now feels like the "wilderness years" of her long periods off work, spells in hospital, and awful stories of being terrorised by hallucinations. I do remember particularly that Laura began to neglect her appearance. She would look scruffy; her hair would be lank and clearly unwashed. But one of the main things I remember is the way she would increasingly look upwards and to the left or right as she was talking to you. As some of her friends and colleagues got to understand her better, we realised that this was because the voices were interrupting her thoughts and concentration. Although Laura still worked in my team, we moved offices, and the nature of our work changed. There was still the short term front line child protection work, but there was more of the longer-term work with families, and because this coincided with a decline in her mental health, I thought at the time that it might have been a contributory factor. But now I'm not sure that anything environmental would have stopped the decline in her mental health.

From time to time, Laura would talk about or make some enquiries about returning to her disaster support work. But this time she would be an independent worker, and it seemed there were too many obstacles to this being a possibility, and not being part of a church further limited her opportunities. I honestly don't know whether this would have been a good idea or whether, in reality, the moment was gone for her. Perhaps she was yearning for a time in her life, or a period in her mental health, when she felt alive and in control. Maybe she missed being in a position of responsibility and respect, and the ability to hold to a belief that she was doing something positive and practical to improve the lives of others.

I was so worried about Laura those next few years. We saw each other, I would say, quite often. I visited her at home, in the hospital, or we would meet for coffee. I knew she was causing herself serious injury through burning herself, and she wouldn't always get medical attention. I couldn't imagine how horrifying and frightening it was for her to see snakes and giant spiders, and I found myself feeling helpless and frustrated, at times, when I knew she wasn't taking her medication. On one occasion, I contacted her allocated community mental health nurse, and on another I phoned her parents, both times against Laura's express wishes. But I felt out of my depth, and actually, I felt it wasn't fair for me to carry the worry on my own. What if she seriously injured or killed herself?

I am not proud to say that I found Laura pretty hard work during this period; she was a shadow of her former self, talking even more than usual in riddles or barely able to engage in conversation. I was never sure how much the other people in her life knew or were supporting her. Laura was, not surprisingly, very flat emotionally, and I knew that not having Blaze living with her, and her guilt over the break of her marriage, weighed heavily on her. I would just feel so relieved when I knew her parents were staying with her. Even though she might burn herself, I thought it was unlikely she would actually kill herself while they were there. Laura would try to conceal her burns, but sometimes she would wince if I hugged her, or wear a long-sleeved shirt on a hot day, and I knew she had been at it again and that she would refuse to get medical treatment. On one occasion, Laura said that she only had to keep going for X number of years. When I asked why, she said because then Blaze would be sixteen and old enough to make her own way in the world, just as Laura had at that age. I remember telling her that Blaze would still be a child at sixteen, and even if she was an adult, she would still carry those emotional scars and the guilt of her mother's death/suicide with her all her life.

I am not sure of the sequence of events, but over the next few years, Laura had numerous periods off work and many meetings with Human Resources. In the early days, I supported Laura at meetings with HR, but as time went on, this became increasingly difficult as I tried to balance my role within the department with my personal relationship with her. Eventually I said I could no longer do it and voiced that she needed to be supported by a colleague or someone from outside work. On individual, departmental, and local authority levels, she was let down. The very profession that is supposed to be all about empathy and support and non-discriminatory practice treated her terribly. If she was assessed as being well enough to return to work by a doctor, that view was rejected by managers. I could see the dilemma from an employer's perspective, but to keep her on paid "garden leave" for two years, when she wanted to work and was declared fit to do so, was really hard for her and unfair. Her employer made it really difficult for her to be redeployed within the authority; he offered her positions that were not suited to her skills and qualities, and then put pressure on her to accept a post or risk being dismissed outright. I hope I helped her a little bit at times with advice on how she might respond, but largely Laura fought this battle alone. Even when she was really unwell, she managed to attend meetings or have conversations with people, and you have to admire her for that. It was clear the employer really wanted Laura gone but realised that they couldn't legally dismiss her. If she had tried to push for early retirement on ill health grounds, I suppose they might have found a way to pay her off—but she was made of stronger stuff!

And then there was the courageous decision Laura made to pursue a complaint against the individual and the church organisation that had abused her when she had been at her most vulnerable. No resolution was achieved, but that was through lack of evidence rather than any suggestion that it hadn't actually happened.

What amazing strength of character Laura has! Everything that the church, some individuals, the health authority, and her employer have thrown at her, she has overcome. Laura and I spoke recently about her feelings of guilt about certain things in her life. But we who know her feel the same: we should have known more, understood more, helped more. But what is great about Laura is that she doesn't bear grudges and she doesn't judge. Laura is a thoroughly good person and friend. She deserves to be happy and fulfilled in her personal and professional life, and I do feel that although her life may not tick all her boxes, she is now as much at ease as I have ever known her to be.

Surrendered

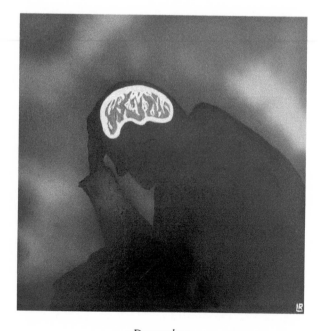

Despondent

CHAPTER FIVE
LOCKED UP!

"Don't piss me off or I'll stop taking my pills and nobody wants that . . . DO THEY?!"

Unknown

Torment

I HAVE HAD THREE HOSPITAL admissions to an acute psychiatric ward.

In a report undertaken by my psychiatrist in 2016, she states that my hospital admissions were as follows:

June 2011 due to auditory hallucinations and suicidal ideation.

January 2012 due to risk of impulsive actions and suicidal intentions.

September 2013 due to acute psychosis with worsening hallucinations and non-compliant with medication. Has acted on commands from voices.

Since my own hospital admission, I have been on psychiatric wards as a professional within my working capacity. However, I want to write this chapter from the perspective of a patient, drawing from my experiences within the ward where I remained a patient. In doing so, I can only tell the story of one hospital stay between the years of 2011 to 2013, and I would like to say that it is not necessarily indicative of all psychiatric wards in the land, or even of that same ward today. When I go on the ward today, albeit as a professional, I do not witness the same practice. And I equally understand that from a patient's perspective it can be and remains to be a traumatizing ordeal in itself. Here I would like to tell you about the first time I was admitted on an acute psychiatric ward, and what life is really like behind locked doors.

PRE-ADMISSION

In the lead-up to admission, I had been to see my GP because I was suffering from depression. In the consultation, she said, "I see many people with depression, and you appear to be experiencing more than standard depression." She asked me if I was hearing voices, if I was suicidal. I did not respond to those questions. She asked these questions and advised me there were long gaps in my speech and I appeared distracted. The GP concluded the consultation by increasing the dose of the antidepressant I was taking, and she said she was going to make a referral to the Community Mental Health Team so I could see a psychiatrist. After a few weeks, I wasn't getting better and went back to the GP to see if the dose of the antidepressant could be increased further. I was told I was on the highest recommended dose of that particular medication, and there was nothing further she could do. She told me that I needed to wait for the appointment with the psychiatrist. Weeks went by, and before that appointment materialized, I found myself admitted to hospital on an acute psychiatric ward.

ARRIVAL

When I entered the ward my first thoughts were, *Where am I? Why am I here?* I felt totally disorientated and confused. It was weird and I had no frame of reference for it. You do not know in advance what you are entering into. No one informs you of what it is going to be like. You just discover what life inside is like as you go along.

When I was admitted, I came via the A&E department at our local hospital. At A&E I was put into a side room where I waited for hours before someone came to see me. I cannot remember how I got to be in A&E in the first place. That's the thing: during the time I was unwell, to the point that I needed hospital admission, many things happened that I cannot remember—things I said, things I did, things my memory cannot recall—creating large gaps of lost time.

The ward was separate from the main general hospital, acting as a unit by itself at the rear of the hospital grounds. When I passed through the doors, they were unlocked and then locked again behind me. I was handed over from the medics that saw me in A&E to ward staff. Initially I was taken into one of the clinic rooms. There, my vitals were taken, and I was presented with a questionnaire which was read out to me. Following that, I was taken to my room where I was searched, and the contents of my bag were taken out and examined. Any items that were considered to be dangerous were removed. On this first occasion, there was absolutely nothing confiscated, but on following admissions, cigarette lighters were removed.

The route to admission on the next two occasions is a little clearer in my mind. The second time I was taken to A&E, it was by a friend who had interrupted me making a noose and writing my suicide notes. The third time, my CPN insisted that I required hospital admission. She took me to A&E and left me there. I wandered off back home. The police turned up at my house. I refused to get in their car and allow myself to be transported back to hospital. They called the CPN who came and persuaded me to go in. When I got back at A&E, the doctor wanted to transfer me to a different hospital where the burns unit was, but I refused, so I was then taken to the psychiatric ward.

WHAT DOES THE UNIT LOOK LIKE?

On my ward, each patient had their own bedroom. Each bedroom had an attached toilet and shower room. There was a single bed, a cupboard, a chest of drawers, and a chair. It was a mixed ward, housing both female and male patients. There were two corridors, one on each side of the unit. One corridor had the bedrooms for the men and the other had the bedrooms for the women—at least this appeared to be the general idea. Sometimes, when a room became available, anyone, male or female, entering the unit would go into the available vacant room until they were moved when a room in the correct corridor became vacant. At the top end of each corridor was a small TV room. There was a larger TV room for everyone. In the middle of the unit was the nurses' station which had windows all around it, I guess so they could see what was going on. Also in the central part of the building was a pool table, and the dining area kitted out with tables for four people, and chairs. Off that room was the hatch where we collected our food. There was also a laundry room, a smoking room, and a couple of rooms that were used by the Occupational Therapy (OT) Department. There was also a clinic room and a medication room. Off another corridor, behind a locked door, was a meeting room and a family room which was used when someone had a child visiting. There was also a small gym, but during my time there, no patients were able to use it, although a member of staff used it each lunchtime. From the central room there was a door that went out into the garden. High wired fences surrounded the unit.

STRUCTURE OF THE DAYS

During the first week I was on the ward I rarely came out of my room. I did not want any visitors, either. I did, however, come out for meals and for medication. Food was served four times per day—breakfast, lunch, dinner, and supper. The food was quite stodgy to be honest—heavy on the stomach. After each meal, the medication room was opened. The patients lined up, waiting in turn to be given their pills. I would line up with the others. When you got to the hatch, you were presented with your medication in a small paper pot, and a small pot of water was provided to help the tablets go down. I found I was often asked to open my mouth after I took the pills so the nurse could see that I had swallowed the pills. The first time, I just did what I was told, even though I had no idea what medication I was taking, and there was no explanation about what the tablets were for. At a later point, at the hatch, I enquired about the medication I was about to take, and the nurse abruptly and forcibly told me to just take them, there were others in the line, so hurry up. As well as set times for medication, there were also occasions when a nurse would come up to me with a tablet and told me to take it, simply saying it would help—help me how, I didn't know.

Other than the regime of mealtimes and medication, there wasn't really anything else that happened. You could play pool, watch the TV, sit in the garden, and talk with other patients. There were some jigsaw puzzles but if you got one of those out you had to use the dining tables which needed to be cleared for meal times. Also, there were pieces missing. Finding oneself hanging around and twiddling your thumbs begged the question of *what does one do during the long days?* The answer for me and for many others was to start smoking cigarettes!

OBSERVATIONS

Nursing staff came around with a clipboard ticking everyone off at intervals both day and night. Observations were conducted for me in the first instance every fifteen minutes. Every fifteen minutes someone would find you, sometimes asking if you were okay, and other times just having a look and going on their way. The longer I was in the hospital, the longer the time between the "obs" became. There were also times of the day when someone from the nursing team would come round and take the patients' pulse and blood pressure. I think it was during my second week there that I found myself in the situation of being assigned a member of staff to be by my side 24/7. This lasted for a period of three to four days. When I say "by my side," I literally mean by my side. Everywhere I went, everything I did, someone was with me. I couldn't even do a poo without someone standing beside me, and that's for real. Staff took it in shifts to shadow me, and even through the night I had someone watching me sleep. Why this happened, I was not informed. They even took my shoelaces from my trainers—my feet were then flopping around in my shoes and I kept tripping, so I made my own laces out of reeds from the bushes in the garden. It was during this level of observation that one day I passed out in the garden. I came to, momentarily, three times. The first time, I found myself on my bed with a number of ward staff and paramedics standing around me. The second time, I was in the ambulance. The third time I came to, I was in a hospital clinic room with my minder still with me. I have no memory of coming back to the psychiatric ward. I was later told it was likely that there was something about the combination of the medication I had been prescribed that was not agreeable with me, and therefore, they had made some adjustments.

OTHER PATIENTS

On the second week I was I was told by one of the doctors I needed to get out of my room more and socialise with the other patients. I therefore ventured out of my room. The ward was always full, all beds taken. There was a mixed bunch of people with different diagnoses and symptoms on display. Some were noisy, shouting out; others were quiet, just sitting and staring into space while others were pacing the corridors. Some patients appeared to get on with others, and others started fights with fellow patients. Some patients had sexual relations with other patients, and there were also illegal drugs being used on the ward. The atmosphere at times was chaotic and volatile. "Peaceful" and "therapeutic" are not words I would associate with the time I spent locked up. When I started to interact with others, the first question was always "How many times have you been on a psychiatric ward?" It was almost as if more times being locked up was a badge of honour, at least that was the way it felt. The second question: "What is your diagnosis?" The third question: "What do you do?" My answer to the first and second question was "It's my first time" and "I don't know." As to the third question, I decided that it probably wasn't a good idea to say that I was a senior social worker in child protection, so I told them I was "a cleaner. I clean up other people's messes." I guess, to some degree, that is kind of true!

One day, a fifteen-year-old boy was admitted on ward with his two "minders." The ward is for adults with severe and acute mental illnesses. Children should not come to the ward as patients. Apparently there were no beds on the adolescent units so he was with us while awaiting a free bed in an age-appropriate unit. A situation occurred one afternoon. There was a lady who kept randomly shouting. She got on this lad's nerves to the point he went up to her and shouted back in her face. Both his supervisors jumped on him and brought him to the floor. Nurses ran out of their station and jumped in. It looked like a mass bundle. Patients in the vicinity ran away in all directions. However, I moved in to get a closer look at what was happening. The boy was shouting and kicking, trying to swing his arms. "Get off me," he kept shouting. While some were telling him to calm down, the male lead nurse was shouting at the supervisors to get off him. This male nurse noticed I was watching what was going on. Finally, the boy was able to get up and went to his room to calm down. The next day, the same lead male nurse came to me and told me that those two particular minders would not be coming back, and promised that this type of situation would not happen again. I was somewhat taken aback that he had called me aside to tell me this. After all, I was but a patient, and no other patients had been informed of the same thing. I can only guess that, because the staff knew my occupation, they were worried that I might speak out and take some form of action over the incident. I don't know.

On another occasion, the jungle drums started beating among us patients because a new gentleman had arrived, "Mr. Broadmoor," as he was named. This chap was an older man and had at some point in his life been an inmate of Broadmoor high-security psychiatric hospital for the criminally insane. These days we would refer to it as a specialist psychiatric forensic hospital. I found Mr. Broadmoor to be an incredibly interesting man. The two of us hit it off, and we spent day after day from breakfast to supper talking together. To be honest, it was mainly him talking about his life. He was a murderer and told me all about it. I also heard his tales of life inside Broadmoor. I didn't reveal much about myself at all, but that didn't seem to matter. I think he was a bit of a narcissist, and although he did ask me questions about myself, I think he liked the air of mystery around me. He was an intelligent man and we talked on many topics. After the fact, I can remember thinking that the I time spent with him was *gold*; that is, no amount of training sessions would give me such insight as these one on one daily interactions with him.

As time went on, I found myself identifying with the others I was locked up with. Although on one hand I was a professional, my mentality began to change. While I was there, there were a couple of escape attempts. One morning a young male patient scaled the fence and did a runner. Rather than thinking, *Oh, no! I hope this fellow will be okay and he will be bought back safely soon! He really isn't very well,* in fact, I thought, *Yeah, go for it, boy!* and I wondered how far he would get before the police caught him. As the hours went by and he still hadn't returned, there was almost an air of excitement among us all thinking he may have been successful in his escape.

STAFF

During my first admission, staff were not dressed in uniform. Personally, I found it difficult to work out who were staff and who were patients. Soon after arrival I observed a young woman playfully interacting with an older woman. It escalated and got a bit out of hand, and the older woman walked off. I was later to find out the older woman was, in fact, one of the ward staff.

In the weeks I was there I can only remember two occasions when a member of staff sat down and talked with me, asking me how I was doing. If they were not busy, they seemed to congregate in the nurses' station, talking among themselves. There were a number of times when I found them to be abrupt and rude to patients, and often shouting at them. One afternoon, two members of staff brought a male patient out into the garden in a wheelchair. The patient, who had limited abilities physically as well as in speech, threw himself out of his wheelchair onto the ground to pick up a discarded cigarette butt and puffed on it to get the remains going again. The two staff members just laughed at him and made jokes at his expense, eventually getting him back up into the chair.

On a Friday or Saturday night, staff would often get themselves either a Chinese or Indian takeaway. The smell wafted through the corridors. It smelled good. They never asked any of the patients if we wanted to get a takeaway in.

There appeared to me to be a somewhat unhealthy culture among the staff, although I did think there were a few good nurses there, too.

SEEING A DOCTOR

When I started to feel I was getting better, I asked to leave. I was told I couldn't. I asked a second time if I could leave. A while later, a doctor and one of the nurses came to speak with me. I had been admitted as an informal/voluntary patient so, in theory, I was within my rights to go home. Basically, they threatened me. They told me that if I insisted on leaving, they would have me "sectioned" and that I "wouldn't want that to happen." During the conversation, they said this more than once. To be honest, I didn't really know what they meant at that time because I received no explanation, but the way they said it didn't sound good. There were other occasions when this threat was made both on this admission and on following admissions. No one could tell me how long I was going to be in hospital, no timeline (timescale) was ever provided, and there appeared to be no end in sight. Talk about the feeling of being locked up and the key being thrown away!

One morning early on in my admission, a nurse came to my room and asked me to come with her because the doctor wanted to see me. I followed her into a part of the unit where I had not been before. The door was opened and before me was a room with a large table surrounded by many people all looking at me as I entered. I sat down and the doctor introduced himself. Each person in turn around the table also introduced themselves. It became all a bit overwhelming within seconds; I couldn't remember who anyone was or why we were there. When the meeting concluded, I thought to myself, *What was that all about?* To this day, although I can remember being taken aback by the event, I still can't imagine what went on, why there were so many people, and who they were. It remains a mystery.

There were other times when I saw a doctor, often a different one, and I can't remember any of their names. They would come and talk to me in my bedroom, sitting on my bed with a member of the ward staff. Sometimes they would see me in the small TV room.

VISITORS

Relatives and friends who come to visit are permitted to come on ward in the afternoon and early evening. The first week, as I have said, I did not want any visitors. I did not want people I knew to see me like that. After the first week, I agreed to a small group of people I considered to be friends and family to visit. There was an occasion when my daughter visited, and we were provided with a small room off the main unit. Although I am aware I did have visitors, my memory of these events is somewhat incomplete. My sister tells me she visited with me on a number of occasions. But I have no memory of her visiting at all, and I certainly have no memory of the content of our conversations, even though she has said they were quite significant.

LEAVE

I was aware that some patients were able to leave the ward for short periods of time to go to the shop, after being given permission to do so. In asking if I could go, I was informed that I was "not allowed." In all fairness, the shop the others were going to was very close to my house, but I wasn't even able to go to the little shop in the main part of the hospital. I struggled to understand why it was that they were allowed out and I was not. Again, no explanation was ever provided for this.

ORGANISED ACTIVITIES

There were two occasions when I was invited to see an OT. Both occasions were one-on-one sessions. The first time, I was asked if I wanted to do "some colouring in." Because I stated that I could draw, I was given a blank A4 sheet of paper and a pencil. On the second occasion, I was taken into a small kitchen and I made scrambled egg on toast under supervision. Other than that, there was no other time whereby I was engaged in any meaningful activity, if that is indeed what you would call it!

PARLOUR GAMES

Boredom on ward is a daily reality. When I was more "with it," I organised some of the other patients by encouraging them to join with me in playing some games. One afternoon I arranged a pool tournament. I recruited a number of patients for this, one of whom we barely saw as he rarely came out of his room except for the odd game of pool. The tournament lasted much of the afternoon. A friend who had visited me had bought me a box of chocolates and, as I hadn't opened them, they became the prize for the winner.

Another time I thought it would be a good idea to play hide and seek. We had a volunteer to be the seeker and the rest of us hid in the grounds. Unfortunately, it didn't really work out. The guy who was the seeker forgot what he was doing—that was a symptom of his current mental state. He wandered off, forgetting about the rest of us, and sometime later I came out of my hiding spot realising things were not going according to plan. Our game of hide and seek also provided "fun" for the nurse who was on observation duty, because she couldn't see all the hiders!

I tried out a few parlour games with varying success. There was no entertainment, so I thought we might as well provide our own.

DISCHARGE

Out of the blue one day I was suddenly told, "You can go home now." I asked, "What? Right now?" They replied, "Yes, you can." It came from nowhere. It was a bit of a shock. I had been in the hospital for a month. I was told that over the next few days the "Crisis Team" would be in touch with me. I packed my bag and was let out.

When I got home was when it hit me. I had a flood of emotions. While in hospital I felt numb, disconnected, and had to learn quickly to adapt to my environment. Now I was back in my home setting, and I felt all at sea. I cried and took myself off to be alone. When the pair from the Crisis Team came to see me that evening, they took me in their car back to the hospital. I saw one of the doctors and a lead nurse. When they spoke to me, they offered for me to be re-admitted, but I declined and was allowed to go back home. I was actually experiencing a delayed emotional response to my experiences of being locked up, rather than a relapse in my mental health.

Despite all I have mentioned, there is much of my experience of life on an acute psychiatric ward that I cannot remember. Months later, I was in the supermarket and a woman came up to me and told me I looked well. I looked at her thinking, *Who is she?* She identified herself as one of the nurses from the ward who had cared for me. I genuinely had absolutely no memory of her.

Life on a psychiatric ward is a mixed bag of experiences and emotions. You are there because you are considered to be acutely mentally unwell. You are often there because you are believed to be a danger either to yourself or to others. Life at that time can be scary as you are tormented by symptoms attributed to your mental illness—in my case, that of my voices. When I was told I had to go to a psychiatric hospital and was threatened that if I did not go with them I would "be sectioned," I felt overwhelmed and powerless. When I was led through the doors, I felt dumped and locked up. Well, I was locked up. I couldn't get out. And when you are there, there can be fearful moments witnessing behaviours of others who are also mentally unwell, and it is a great challenge to remain among these people. If you think going to this type of hospital is for "a break," you are so wrong. I found myself with the limited resources I had left inside me, having to fight to be able to breathe.

Years later at a hearing voices support group, I met others who had been admitted to the same acute psychiatric ward. One in the group described that ward as "being worse than being in prison," and he went on to say, "the environment is toxic," and he wasn't too complimentary about the staff and the manner in which they practiced, either. He was able to compare it with prison, because he had been in prison.

Due to the nature of mental health, one can never predict what will happen in the future. But I do hope I will never have to go back to having further hospital admissions.

Angels and Demons

Demon Possession vs. Mental Health—Africa

CHAPTER SIX
FAITH CAN MOVE MOUNTAINS

"The Devil whispered in my ear,
'You're not strong enough to withstand the storm.'
Today I whispered in the Devil's ear,
'I AM THE STORM.'"

Unknown

Battle for the Soul

WHEN I WAS IN BURKINA Faso, in October 1987, we drove off into the bush one morning to visit what was called "The Village of Healing." In this remote community, those who were able would work in the field, tending to the crops in the mornings, and during the afternoons they went round praying for the sick, one by one. The majority of those unwell were considered to be demon possessed. Some had been walked to the village, travelling miles, delivered there by family members. Under the trees in the shade, people lay on mats. They were mostly women. Some of these women had their babies sitting next to them. What was shocking was that they lay there with one foot through a hole in the centre of a large log that was pinned by a stake close to the ankle to prevent the foot coming out of the log. There were logs that also had chains bound around them and they were tied to a tree. Some of these unwell people had one log attached, while others two—one log for each foot. The explanation for this, we were told, was when people come to the village, the demons inside them are really strong and the sufferers need restraining to prevent them from harming themselves or others. Some could be violent because of the strength of the demons. We were told a story of a lady who, after prayer, was let out of the log as she was believed to have been made well, but the demon within her had not gone. She got a knife and murdered her baby sitting next to her. The information provided was that the stronger the demon, the more logs and chains were required. Even when the demons were believed to have left that person, the individual still remained bound for a period of time, to make sure the demons were gone before the person was set free.

Was this a cultural difference in caring for those with mental health struggles, or was it actually as they said it was, about delivering and exorcising people from demonization and possession? Whatever it was, I thought it was a bit on the scary side. The images I saw that day have remained with me as I try to make sense of them. Why am I telling you that story? I think because when you have witnessed something like that, which is a bit on the extreme side, and, when issues surrounding mental health come to mind, it causes me to think, *Does what I see have anything to do with mental health? I'm not like those women, am I?* I didn't want to be considered to be one of those "poor souls." I think my western mind had interpreted what I saw as mental health. However, to an African mind, it is definitely about demon possession. Maybe I shouldn't have debated this.

Maybe the two issues are totally separate. Maybe cultural difference and understanding has got in the way? Questions arise of how others might treat me, not that I thought I would be taken to the woods and tied to a tree, but it's all relative, isn't it?

I was extremely interested to discover that the Human Rights Watch in October 2020 have produced a report about people with mental health conditions living in chains. *Living in Chains—Shackling of People with Psychosocial Disabilities Worldwide* advises by a means of an introduction that: "Hundreds of thousands of people with mental health conditions are shackled around the world . . . Men, women, and children, some as young as ten, are chained or locked in confined spaces for weeks, months, and even years, in about sixty countries across Asia, Africa, Europe, The Middle East, and the Americas." Human Rights Watch have also launched a campaign called #breakthechains to end the practice of shackling. You can find out more information and read the full report on hrw.org. This report has been published thirty-three years after what I witnessed while in West Africa in 1987.

The issues surrounding mental health and spirituality are of great interest to me. Given my lifestyle and work prior to my engagement with mental health services, it is no wonder. As a missionary and a minister of twenty years, within the Christian faith, it was the sum of my entire life. My thoughts and actions were shaped and led by the strengths, and maybe even my weaknesses, too.

It is my belief that the relevance of spirituality and religion within the context of mental health is one that should not be ignored or swept under the carpet. There appears to be a distinct difference between Western, Eastern, African, and tribal understandings of the interface between spirituality and mental health, mental illness, mental distress, and mental disorders. Because I live in the United Kingdom, the fluctuating state of my mental health has been defined by psychiatric interpretations of our Western thinking. I suggest that the framework provided that presents us with the classification and diagnosis of "what is mad" and "who is mad" is a cultural framework. This leads me to question whether the current paradigm presented in the medical model, with the additions provided in a psycho-social model, are complete. It causes me to consider other potential dynamics which could be in play. In the field of mental health, social workers talk about having a person-centred, holistic approach which is led by the service user; but I do wonder if that is truly the case, since we are all so greatly influenced by social norms. These norms, the commonly agreed-on state of being "normal," are presented to us with a box called "normality." Services and interventions are provided to bring us back to a place of normality and we are told what the acceptable form of normality is. We are given medication to make us "normal." We are engaged in talking therapy to make us "normal." Surely there is more to it than that? I would suggest there should be no limits, as all things are possible.

WHAT IS SPIRITUALITY AND RELIGION?

Definitions are important in helping us understand conceptions, dimensions, and phenomena. There are many forms of religion and spirituality, beliefs and faith, so there are many people that draw on these for alternative help, to create hope and find meaning when faced with problems. As some may draw upon traditional medicines that have been passed down through generations that can be of benefit, so too are other alternatives considered and engaged in.

The *Collins Dictionary* tells us that "Religion is the belief in and worship of a superhuman controlling power, especially a personal God or gods. A religion is a particular system of belief in a God or gods and the activities that are connected with this system. It is a pursuit or interest followed with great devotion." Definitions from *Oxford Languages* tells us that "Spirituality is the quality of being concerned with the human spirit or soul as opposed to material or physical things. Spirituality has to do with a person's spirit, soul and inner life."

In making a distinction between the two, we are informed that "religion is a personal set or institutionalized system of attitudes, beliefs, and practices" (Merriam-Webster.com). Christina Puchalski, MD, director of the George Washington Institute for Spirituality and Health, contends that "spirituality is the aspect of humanity that refers to the way individuals seek and express meaning and purpose and the way they experience their connectedness to the moment, to self, to others, to nature, and to the significant or sacred."

In looking at the relationship between religion and spirituality, the University of Minnesota in the United States of America (website: www. takingcharge.csh.umn.ed/what-spirituality), suggests:

"While spirituality may incorporate elements of religion, it is generally a broader concept. Religion and spirituality are not the same thing, nor are they entirely distinct from one another. Spirituality is a broad concept with room for many perspectives. In general, it includes a sense of connection to something bigger than ourselves, and it typically involves a search for meaning in life. People may describe a spiritual experience as sacred or transcendent or simply a deep sense of aliveness and interconnectedness. Some may find that their spiritual life is intricately linked to their association with a church, temple, mosque, or synagogue. Others may pray or find comfort in a personal relationship with God or a higher power. Still others seek meaning through their connections to nature or art. Like your sense of purpose, your personal definition of spirituality may change throughout your life, adapting to your own experiences and relationships."

Religious and spiritual examples—prayer, worship, engagement with others in the religious community, meditation, visualisations, dreams, spirit helpers, guardian angels, animal spirit helpers, ceremonies, rituals, tarot cards, oracle cards, spiritualism, mysticism, witchcraft, occult (not an exclusive list)—are tapped into by individuals and groups all over the world.

Christianity, Judaism, Islam, Buddhism, Hinduism, Sikhism, Taoism, Baha'i, Paganism—again, not an exclusive list of world religions—give shape to many a belief.

Religion and spirituality can be two separate entities. But there can be and often is a massive overlap in the relationship between the two. An example of this is that there are those that would identify with and call themselves a Christian, but they do not see themselves as being religious, but rather spiritual. Typically, today, many talk about having a personal relationship with God. There are those who, to varying degrees, have confidence in an existence of God. Some believe in this personal relationship while others believe there is a higher power out there. Most who do believe in a god or spiritual power believe there to be a connection that is made with that being and our lives, our affairs, and influence on the world around us. This interaction changes and develops over time. It has movement, is active and dynamic. Many feel the presence of God in their daily lives. There are times when people feel close to God, times when people get angry with God and blame him for the wrongs in their lives and for devastating situations that take place in the world, especially at times of disaster, and there are times when people reject God.

FAITH

Faith is a living, breathing entity. Faith grows. Although our personal level of faith may be small, we can connect with a state of faith that is without bounds.

Biblical faith, as defined in Hebrews 11: 1, states, "Now faith is the assurance of things hoped for, the conviction of things not seen." In examining the extraordinary phenomenon of the concept of faith, I believe there are four key elements to be considered:

1) Faith in God's character—He is who he says he is.

2) Faith in God's sovereignty—He can do what he says he can do.

3) Faith in your position—I am who God says I am.

4) Faith in Christ in you—I can do what God says I can do.

If we are to fully grasp faith in its fullness, it has the power to move mountains. We can have confidence and authority that transcends our earthly existence into realms that are on a higher plane. We can move from the natural to the supernatural. Our insight not only expands but is transformed in the light of the presence of a higher being. Faith comes through a loving personal relationship with God. Faith connects with our own inner spirit. For Christians, we are inspired by and receive inspiration from the Holy Spirit. It is a force that we are moved by. There is an internal stirring and moving, which leads to external movement. This inspiration comes from our understanding, knowledge, and revelation we receive from the word of God, the Holy Scriptures, the Bible. Faith develops in us through hearing. That is the secret of biblical faith—that we hear, hear from the word of God. In this place, we find He is all-sufficient. Faith that comes from the heart "always produces a definite change, a definite experience, in those that profess it" (Prince, 1986). There is a unique quality about faith. In the context of being faced with mental illness, faith opens the door to dynamic possibilities.

RELIGION VS. SCIENCE

The religion/spirituality/faith versus science debate is a longstanding one. There are some who laugh at me when I say I am a creationist, not an evolutionist. Historically, those who have looked to science to offer explanations over that of religion were branded as heretics. Today, those who look at the faith in a situation over that of science are branded as nutters. The pendulum has swung, but there remains conflict between the two. Complexities arise because there is a lack of understanding and an air of mystery in both camps. Scientists don't know everything. Theologians don't know everything. This presents us with numerous and uncertain dilemmas. When faced with mental illness, we can find that both the scientific evidence and understanding, and the perspectives of a living and active faith, are challenged. Finding a way through the mist that is generated can be difficult. The interface between these two seemingly opposing views appears to be somewhat complex. Regardless of the brain strain, we must find a way forward, and maybe the two can even live in harmony.

HELPFUL AND HARMFUL

It is widely considered that for someone to have a good quality of life, our physical and mental health both need to be in top shape. With respect to our mental health, it can either deteriorate over time or somewhat rapidly. There may be a number of factors for this: stress, trauma, a disposition, our genes, and sometimes you just cannot put your finger on the reason why. When confronted with ill health, whether we are in a place of crisis or we are learning to cope with symptoms that we live with on a daily basis, we can identify our spiritual strengths in aiding us. This can help us cope with situations we are faced with, and it can assist in resolving problems and underpin our state of well-being.

Religion, to some degree, can be part of the problem, limiting our thoughts and actions, giving us unnecessary guilt, restraining us. It could also be part of the solution, providing us with support, comfort, and even healing. It is up to us to consider how our lives are being affected by our spiritual and religious beliefs in helping make sense of our experiences and the role they can play as we move forward into a place of recovery. As far as mental health services are concerned, interventions leading to what is called "recovery," are the view and approach that are given the thumbs up.

When considering our spiritual influences, needs, assets, and goals, we can not only find encouragement but also a path to move forward on. A religious group can provide its members with a sense of belonging, having shared beliefs and experiences. It provides a sense of community. It may also provide pastoral care. Our religious and spiritual beliefs can be a source of comfort and strength. Our faith can provide us with increased hope and an optimistic outlook. Our spiritual beliefs can provide us with a sense of purpose and meaning for our lives.

EXORCISMS AND THE DELIVERANCE MINISTRY

Exorcism is a fascinating topic. It has captured the imagination of Hollywood, and movies have been made that feature this. Hollywood can be very different from reality, though. The causes of how a person said to become afflicted with evil spirits or demons are varied. There are even those who believe that what some call mental illness is in fact demonic activity. People of all beliefs and faith groups can believe that mental illnesses are demon possession. In Arabic, the word for madness is *jinoon*, which came out of the word *jinn*, meaning evil spirits. The "jinn spirits" play a role in and are factors when something goes wrong or is not right, like ill health. A number of religions perform exorcisms. Today within Christian circles, the preferred term for this is deliverance or the deliverance ministry. My personal experience and understanding comes through my Christian faith, and it is from that basis that my views on this subject have been formed. Should one not be afraid to look at this subject beyond that of textbooks and look into how people of all religions and forms of spirituality come face to face with the demonic, it would be gripping stuff.

In 2018 the Vatican announced new training courses to be held to meet the increased demand for exorcisms. The Anglican Church has also trained and appointed people in this form of ministry as have many other denominations. It is the opinion of many that there is a place for the deliverance ministry in the twenty-first century, and it is believed that the demand for it is on the rise. There are those within church and faith groups who deny the existence of evil spirits, of the demonic altogether. If one is to embark into exorcism/deliverance today, it is encouraged by some groups for a medical assessment to be provided by a doctor of medicine before any prayer of this nature gets underway. I would also advocate for there to be understanding and consent on the behalf of the recipient. However, although this would be a sensible approach to safeguard the vulnerabilities of an individual, not all of those practising within the deliverance ministry would necessarily take this route. There are some church groups, especially within evangelical and charismatic circles, where deliverance is a standard form of prayer like any other.

Here in the UK, when it comes to children, it is my opinion that deliverance/exorcisms, should be considered a "no go" area. Social Services, the police, and the courts will act if "a child is suffering or is likely to suffer significant harm" (Section 47, Children Act 1989). It would be considered, therefore, a form of child abuse. For adults, however, the potential risks involved fall into more of a grey area, although we do have legislation that safeguards vulnerable adults.

At one time in my ministry years, I was trained in the deliverance ministry and even took part in exorcisms. Within this ministry, I have prayed with individuals, I have been present during group sessions, and I have dealt with "unholy spirits" that have lurked in the darkness elsewhere. I have witnessed the manifestations of demon powers in the form of shaking, speaking, shouting, screaming, laughing, vomiting, drooling, and spitting. Exorcism can be a noisy affair, but as some go loudly, others go quietly. When I moved into my own house, I felt there was a spirit, a ghost as it were, in the corner of the living room in the front of the house. I cast that spirit out, and I believe it has gone, as it has not bothered me since. There was a night when I was in a sleeper carriage on an overnight train in Romania. Shortly after lights-out, I saw a ghost in the form of a man. I said aloud, "what are you doing there?" I rolled over and went to sleep on the other side with my back to it. I have myself received the deliverance ministry. I have to say though, in my case, either "the exorcist" wasn't very good, or the demons were not there in the first instance. In having first-hand experience, there were times when I wondered what is the appropriate use of this form of ministry. There is not a demon behind every lamppost.

Definitions that consider demon possession, demonization, and demon oppression can provide us with some differing levels of understanding. Possession: being taken over from within, like a form of ownership. Demonization: being affected or influenced by. Oppression: by a force from outside of us. The issue of curses would fall into this last bracket.

There are some today who consider schizophrenia to be demonic possession which is to be "treated" by exorcism. *Pigs in the Parlor: A Practical Guide to Deliverance*, an American publication, was for some a key text in the healing and deliverance ministry during the '70s and '80s. In this book, there is a whole chapter dedicated to schizophrenia. The authors believed to have had "special revelations" on this subject and how to deal with it. They describe schizophrenia as "a nest of demon spirits." In continuing their belief on this topic, they talk about "dual personalities." They go on to say, "The control demon of schizophrenia invites the other demons in, in order to cause the distortion of personality. Schizophrenia ALWAYS begins with 'rejection.' It commonly begins in childhood or infancy and sometimes while the child is yet in the mother's womb. There are many causes for rejection. Perhaps the child was not wanted. It may have been the wrong sex desired by the parents . . . Schizophrenia can be demonically inherited . . . The demons pick out one or more of her children to feed down through."

In dealing with this "nest of demons" the authors instruct that; ". . . these demonic spirits in the schizophrenic must be separated, cast out, and given up." You can see the teachings of one of the authors himself on YouTube. Although this text was written in the early 1970s, this understanding on the theme of schizophrenia continues to be believed by some today. In the first instance, people with schizophrenia do not have a split, dual, or multiple personalities. This is a myth and false notion. It has been a common misunderstanding through lack of knowledge and ignorance. Hallucinations that are experienced by the schizophrenic are not multiple personalities. This misconception of what schizophrenia is about puts a crack in the foundations of the belief that has been built on top of it. Equally, I am not convinced that the doorway opened by rejection in this context lets a host of demons enter into a person's life. Rejection is considered by many within the deliverance ministry as a "demonic squatter" and can be addressed through this ministry in setting people free. Although there remains an element of our level of knowledge of schizophrenia being incomplete, and you could say there is a sense of mystery around the illness, it is still defined as a mental illness. I know some in the deliverance ministry still practice from this base in dealing with schizophrenia. I hope that we have moved on not only from the perspective of understanding the illness but also in the spiritual context associated with it.

I have also heard a tale of someone I once knew who came out of a deliverance session with bruises because she had been struck by the person delivering this form of prayer ministry. I would call that physical assault. The British evangelist, Smith Wigglesworth (1859–1947), hit, punched, or slapped people, or the afflicted part of the body, during the course of his healing ministry. It is well recorded that he saw his style as one that dealt with the evil forces behind the affliction. Therefore, he believed he was hitting the demonic spirit, not the person. He was known as "the man who punched out the demons" (christianitytoday.com). It is also believed he had great success in dealing with the demonic. I do not wish to criticise this man, as his ministry is considered to have been key in the history of the church during the 20th century, particularly within the beginnings of the Pentecostal movement. However, I feel if people are trying to imitate his style of ministry in this way today, it is not acceptable behaviour.

This form of ministry can bring with it much harm and many dangers. It can cause great psychological and spiritual damage. The attempt to perform exorcisms can also have the opposite effect and make the mental health of the recipient worse.

Healing can take place in three ways.

1) It can occur naturally, as the human body has the ability to repair itself.

2) Through medicine and medical interventions, healing can be administered by skilled individuals. Traditional and alternative methods may also be deployed.

3) I would also suggest there can be divine healing which takes place through a supernatural occurrence.

From a biblical perspective within the Christian faith, we are told that when Jesus died on the cross, it was not only for our sins but also our sicknesses, as "by His stripes we are healed" (Isaiah 53:5). It was also at the cross where Jesus defeated Satan, the Devil, Lucifer, Diabolos, or whatever else you wish to call him, as he has a number of names, along with his host of demons. It is good to be aware of the pitfalls associated with the deliverance ministry and exorcisms and to be mindful of the potential for harm. Despite this, there remains a call for this form of ministry today. There are cases where it has been considered by the recipients that the outcome has been a success. In Jesus' own ministry, it is well recorded that He cast out demonic powers which resulted in individuals being set free and knowing its healing power. For exorcism within the Christian faith in the deliverance ministry, the focus is on the power of Jesus, as it is in Him where we find the victory. The exorcist must have confidence that he/she has a great power at work in them through Jesus, more than that of demonic beings. Overwhelmingly, the purpose of the deliverance ministry and exorcism is to bring about freedom.

SPIRITUAL ABUSE

Because there can be abuse that takes place within the deliverance ministry, spiritual abuse can take a number of forms. In child protection, abuse is defined in four categories:

1) Physical abuse.

2) Sexual abuse.

3) Emotional abuse.

4) Neglect.

As with children, so can any one of these four categories affect the lives of adults. I would like to highlight a fifth form of abuse that is not listed or recognised as a category in its own right—that of spiritual abuse within the Christian church and other forms of religion and spirituality.

Spiritual abuse. What is it? In the first instance, abuse is a misuse of power. The power usurped by one person over another can be manipulative and controlling as well as downright harmful. It uses people for the gains and gratifications of another. The misuse of power is a betrayal and as a result, trust is broken and even destroyed. In the misuse of power, victims are formed. The damage done and the harm caused can last a lifetime. Some find a place of healing and others do not. In cases of spiritual abuse, it is more often that it is the church leaders that are the guilty ones, the perpetrators. Parishioners place their trust in their spiritual leaders. Spiritual leaders are "shepherds of the flock." Their purpose is to care for and lead "the sheep." This is the role of a pastor. Although all Christian leaders do not have the gift and are not appointed as pastors—some are evangelists, prophets, teachers, and apostles—it is the case that the spiritual leader points others towards God, that he/she shows the goodness and love of the heavenly father. Leaders are only human. They have their own hang-ups and pain. Some seek to fill the void within themselves by striving to make their name known, give their ministry national recognition, be the best, or be the first. In doing this, they may use and abuse others along the way in seeing their vision fulfilled. They lose sight that the role of a spiritual leader is one of servanthood. They are appointed to lead by serving, and not vice versa. If you find the people striving to serve the needs of the leaders, it should ring alarm bells. Jesus washed the feet of his disciples—not the other way round. Through the words and actions that manipulate and control—the misuse of prayer and counselling ministry, ritualistic abuse, emotional abuse, physical abuse, even the sexual abuse by leaders within the church—the effects not only destroy the soul but also damage the spirit of a person. When a grave betrayal of trust and abuse of power takes place, it not only destroys the relationship between the person with the leader, but also the person with God. The person subjected to this form of abuse has an impaired understanding of God through their experience, even though their theological basis may be contrary to that experience. It taints their knowledge of God. Hence, the abuse becomes spiritual.

This form of abuse is not only attributed to cult leaders but also leaders within the local church. Leaders from all denominations are not immune from being perpetrators of this form of abuse. For the person who either experiences this form of abuse first-hand or witnesses it in the life of others, they are presented with a choice of whether they should stay or go. In the going, they are often ostracised by the community that had been a central factor in their life. They lose friendships with those they were once close to, and it can also divide families. I have known people who have been deeply affected by spiritual abuse. Some move on and "try" a different church, with some being unable to settle. Others find a new spiritual home. Others maintain a personal faith but avoid going to church. There are those whose experience has been detrimental to their mental health and have enlisted help from psychiatric services. The sad thing is, people can lose their faith in God altogether. People once fully engaged in church life, even people who have served in leadership teams and have had a significant ministry themselves, now declare themselves to be atheists.

My experience of this kind of abuse was up close and personal. As I have witnessed others hurt and deeply scarred by a church that became toxic with a leader that caused untold pain in many lives, so I was significantly harmed as well.

When my mental health became unstable once again, I was invited to live in the home of leaders from the mission who were also leaders in a local church. I moved in and became part of the family. They had two young children and I became the godmother for one of them. We enjoyed time together, I went on holiday with them and on occasions spent Christmas with them and their wider family. I spent a lot of time with the female leader. In the evenings after the children had gone to bed, she would spend time praying for me.

As time went on, one day she told me she had received revelation that she knew the root of my suffering. She told me I had been sexually abused by my father. She also told me that my mother knew and was covering up for my father. I want to make it clear I was never abused by my father in any way, let alone sexually. I later found out that I was not the only one she had said this to. There were many others who she believed had been sexually abused by one member of their family or another, all of which were untrue reasons for the dis-ease in people's lives. I told her this was not the case, but the more I refused to believe, the more she told me I was, "in denial." She told me that I needed to accept it in order to deal with it, and I wouldn't be made well until I did. This messed with my head; I started having nightmares and the thought of it gave me considerable pain. Over time, it also affected my relationship with my parents. As the years went on, my mental health fluctuated, and on each occasion I was unwell, she would bring the same issue up as the root of my problems.

I am not the most emotional of people. In fact, my emotional responses in situations have been found to be lacking. In the course of recounting these stories, I have mentioned that I have cried. I recall these times of doing so as they are the odd occasions where I have. On the whole, I am not a very emotional person; I am very matter of fact. It is both a blessing and a curse. It makes me good at what I do, as I do not have an emotional connection in the cases I have worked with, but I do have an understanding and empathy. Yet, in personal relationships, it can bring distance, as the other person does not feel I fully understand or care about the situation or the way they feel, and I guess there is an element of truth in that. In the case I'm mentioning, my emotional lack was the evidence that backed up her "revelation." In a prayer session, one on one, she sat on my lap, and while praying, she put her hands all over my body. I became stiff and rigid. I did not like it but felt, since it was done during prayer, that I was unable to push her off. When reflecting on this experience, I do not believe it was sexual abuse nor that she got any pleasure from it. Rather, I believe she was misguided in her methods.

My mental health took a turn for the worse. She assigned me another female member of the leadership team to take care of me, as it was considered I needed daily support. My husband was in agreement as he was unable to cope with me. She took over from where the other leader took off. During the course of my interactions with her over the months and years, she provided much sustenance, but it ended up with her sexually assaulting me. She later confessed that she wanted me exclusively for herself. She even wanted to take me away from my husband. Yes, the police were involved, albeit at a later date. I gave a statement by video in the victim suite at the police station. However, it was my word against hers, and the police investigation concluded with no further action. The church leadership was aware of what had taken place at the time it happened, and they covered it up, only wanting to believe their version of the truth. After they moved from me, they focused on my husband. They said he had "anger issues" that needed to be dealt with.

In leaving, although we tried to leave on good terms, my husband and I lost everything we knew at that time. As we were ourselves leaders in that same church, we lost not only our friends and the community we were part of but also our source of finances. Daily living became difficult. We struggled to feed ourselves; we were unable to pay our mortgage, pay the bills, run a car, and everything else that one often takes for granted. We felt we were left with no option, so we rented out our house, left the country, and moved into a caravan.

We went off grid, into hiding, where we spent the next year. A dear friend, a person with a national/international ministry and influence, came alongside us and offered us a job as youth pastors. We were reluctant at first as we were not keen to be part of a church, let alone involved with the leadership. However, eventually we were persuaded. We agreed to go for a period of six months at the end of which would be a review to give us time to decide whether this really was what we wanted and if we were ready to immerse ourselves in church life again. But we were not ready; we could not shake off the effects of our past experience. There was the additional strain of the ride my husband had been on with my mental illness and substantial cracks in our marriage. We left and returned to our home in Wales.

On our return, we found that we were not welcome. We were even told to leave town. We were advised that there was a fear that we might start a new church that would take away from, and have better youth work, than the one we had left. We had no intention of doing such a thing. We did, however, begin a new life, but my husband took one path and I another. I continued in the ministry as an independent itinerant minister, with oversight from the same dear friend who took us out of the caravan. I became a chaplain and preacher in small Welsh chapels, along with my continued overseas missions, particularly those of post-tsunami work in Sri Lanka. As for my now ex-husband, I don't believe he has ever fully recovered from the combination of the effects of my mental illness and the spiritual abuse that he suffered from.

THE DIAGNOSTIC TOOL AND CULTURAL BELIEFS

When applying the paradigm of the diagnostic tool of ICD-10 (International Classification of Disease produced by the World Health Organisation/WHO) or DSM-IV (*Diagnostic & Statistical Manual of Mental Disorders*, used in the USA), if I was to bring certain well known biblical characters into clinic and sit them down in front of a psychiatrist, what would they make of them?

- Abraham—paranoid schizophrenic?
- Moses—schizoaffective?
- Peter—bipolar?
- Paul—schizoaffective?
- Jesus—schizophrenic, delusions of grandeur?

I think a psychiatrist would have a field day with them all! It is often the case when extreme examples are bought before a psychiatrist, they have to explore the cause and the effect. There can be a struggle in finding meaning. Over the years, there have been those that are dismissive and have been indifferent to a person's religious and spiritual beliefs. Although it can be a challenge, others find value in belief systems that the medical model on some level excludes. The importance of context must be one to be considered. Context is inclusive of beliefs and culture. I believe we must question whether we are experiencing higher realms of spirituality, or the deep dark depths of madness.

Is it possible that voice hearers in our Western society are wrongly observed as being mentally ill? There is an admission that not everyone who hears voices has a mental health problem. Hearing voices can be positive: they may encourage, comfort, bring understanding, give direction. They may be practical and remind you of things you need to do. Voices can also be negative. They can be distressing and frightening, they may threaten you, they may tell you to harm yourself or harm someone else.

Research estimates that about 10 percent of people experience hearing voices. In 70 percent of patients under psychiatric services, the voices are believed to be related to trauma. Stress, worry, lack of sleep, extreme hunger, and recreational and prescribed drugs can all be associated with or are triggers for hearing voices. What about the other 30 percent? Spiritual reasons and beliefs are considered by some as an explanation for the voices people hear. If, therefore, hearing voices is a result of spiritual activity, are we to adopt supernatural means to deal with it?

I have met people from all walks of life—male and female, people of all ages, people of all beliefs and those of no belief, those educated to a higher level and those that are not, those that hold down high-powered jobs and those that are unemployed, those that are financially wealthy and those that live on state benefits, people from different cultures. Many have described spiritual experiences in what has been defined as their psychosis—out-of-body experiences, levitation, hearing the voice of God, hearing the devil's voice, some being specific about which ear they hear which voices, some seeing demons and angels. Some have talked about being raped by or having sexually encountered demons without knowing about Incubuses and Succubus. So-called 'psychotic experiences' that have a spiritual overtone are many.

As hallucinations, visions, and voices can be attributed to spirituality, so can the state of one's mood. Both the highs and lows and states of mania and depression can be attributed to a spiritual connection. If you have moved in similar circles to mine, you may have heard some say, "I'm on a spiritual high."

CONFLICTS OF THINKING

For someone with the mental health diagnosis of schizophrenia/ schizoaffective disorder, it can be difficult to distinguish between that which are encounters within the spirit realm and that which is psychosis. For the past twenty years, I've been trained and served in the Christian ministry, and for the past fifteen years, I have served as a social worker.

There can be a conflict in perspectives and understanding. Fundamental beliefs that underpin both vocations can complement each other. An alliance can be found where core values are shared. At the same time, they can be in conflict with one another. There have been questions that I have wrestled with, questions that have challenged everything I once knew and believed, and questions that challenge the contemporary beliefs of this day and age. There are struggles between understanding that which belongs in the physical realm and that which is of the spiritual realm. Even in that last statement, there are some who would dismiss all ideas and notions of there even being a spirit realm. However, for me, as with others who have religious and spiritual beliefs—i.e., people of faith—the spiritual side of life is not something confined to fairy tales and fantasy. The spiritual realm is just as real as the physical realm. This may be a debated issue for us in the West, yet through my travel in Africa and other parts of the world, there is no debate; it is taken as so. It has led me to question all forms of what is seen and unseen—to question issues around mental health and spirituality and the interface between the two. If we were to say that all forms of what medics call psychosis is mental illness, then are we not branding people of all religions and forms of spirituality as having either impaired cognition or mental disorders? Can we come to a place where there is a harmony that dispels turmoil?

For those who find themselves working with someone where their religion, spirituality, and faith is a central part of their life, then you must cultivate appreciation and respect from a base of empathy that leads to empowerment.

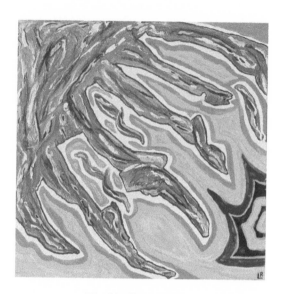

El sol brillia en Bolivia

Water Aid

CHAPTER SEVEN
SOAR WITH EAGLES, ROAR LIKE A LION

"When you have a purpose, a dream, a vision for your life, you can do anything, go anywhere."

Laura Ruth

Beyond the Barricades

THERE WERE TIMES WHEN I was "on a mission," when I was probably experiencing a touch of mania, but that was not always the case. Although

I am not a great planner, I had vision with a goal in mind. There were times when I set out to achieve the ideas I had, bringing them into reality. There were also times that as opportunities presented themselves, I grabbed hold, held tight, and went with the flow of the ride I found myself on, not knowing where it was taking me. I have found when I push through the barricades and obstacles in my own life and go out into the world, that as a Christian, I believe Jesus himself commands us to do so, and He has used the broken fool that I am.

PURPOSE

Each one of us needs a purpose on our life. Our purpose is what makes us alive. Our purpose is the *why* that shapes us, moving us forward hour by hour, day by day. Without a purpose, without a vision, we get sucked into a cycle of despair that destroys and kills our souls. Without a purpose and a vision, we shrivel up and perish. When I have been in the deepest, darkest places of depression, I have held onto that purpose. When I have come face to face with death himself, I have believed in the goodness of what is to come. When everything is black around you, it is certainly not easy. When it is so dark, the smallest flicker of light can be seen, and it is what I have walked towards.

Eleanor Roosevelt said, "You gain strength, courage, and confidence by every experience in which you really stop to look fear in the face. You are able to say to yourself, I lived through this horror. I can take the next thing that comes along."

We are to be encouraged to live life to the fullest. When things have not been well and my struggles have been hard to bear, I have known a certain strength to deal with the strain of the moment. That strength pulls me through. Where we have overcome enemies in our own lives, we have a special gift to come alongside others, to encourage them to fight against the adversaries they face.

A purpose causes us to be able to dream. We are not restricted by the expectations and opinions of others. There are those who believe—as I myself have heard it said—a person with a severe mental health condition is "unstable, unreliable, compromised, limited" in what they can do and achieve. I say to you who pen me in, *I will not wallow like a pig in the mud, I will rise up and fly with the eagles.* A mind with a purpose is unlimited, creative, and brilliant, truly fabulous. When you have a purpose, a dream, a vision for your life, you can do anything, go anywhere. You can expect to see the spark of magic and miracles.

EMOTIONS

The *Collins Dictionary* defines emotions as: "a feeling such as happiness, love, fear, anger, or hatred, which can be caused by the situation that you are in or the people you are with. Emotion is part of a person's character that consists of their feelings, as opposed to their thoughts."

To feel from the heart comes naturally for some, and it is feared by others. One's emotions can be tricky to handle at times. Emotions can be overwhelming and can cripple us, but they can also be liberating. Some people wear their emotions, their heart, on their sleeve, but for others, you have to scratch beneath the surface and dig a bit deeper to uncover them. Emotions can be provoked by what we see in films, in books, in our relationships, engagement with others, in our line of work, our leisure activities. The greatest rush of emotion I have ever felt was my sky dive on my forty-first birthday. It was the best feeling ever!

We must be able to be in touch with our emotions, to have compassion for those who suffer. To be consumed by your emotions, on the other hand, is not healthy. It is not healthy for you as a person, and it is not healthy if you are to be able to effectively minister to others. As there is a place to value and adore one's emotions, there is also a place where they are to be ignored and repressed. We must learn not to be dominated by them; instead, we are to dominate them. Emotions can break us, and emotions can heal us. Emotions can lead us in our responses and actions, but we can harness them, use them, and enjoy them. We must find a balance between our heads and our hearts.

When working in the mission field, you may experience what is called "culture shock." Dictionary.com defines culture shock as a "state of bewilderment and distress experienced by an individual who is suddenly exposed to a new, strange, or foreign social and cultural environment, way of life, or set of attitudes." Culture shock can cause one to feel anxiety, disorientation, isolation, alienation, helplessness, uncertainness, confusion, sadness, loneliness, or extreme homesickness. I have experienced culture shock in reverse. When I have walked into TESCO after a mission overseas, I have stood there in the middle of the first aisle and my jaw has dropped in total bewilderment, overcome with emotions.

We can all be prone to culture shock, and we can all, at times, feel the impact of our emotions in what we come face to face while out in the field. There have been times when I have wondered if I have become desensitised, hard, and emotionless, having gotten used to sights of suffering. I think at times I have forgotten that when taking others with me, my companions may experience overwhelming emotions that they need time to process.

There was an occasion when I had a group with me and we had visited a village in the morning, and we were on our way to visit the next village. As we were travelling between the two places, one of the group members asked if we could stop and take five. My first thought was, *What for?* It then dawned on me. I asked the driver to pull up on the roadside under the next tree to provide us with a bit of shade from the heat of the day. Members of the group had an emotional moment, some having a cry, before gathering themselves and being ready to move on to the next place.

THE WORK PLACE

Being on a mission isn't just about going overseas. It can be that we are "called" to serve our families. A mission can be to bring our children up in a way that shapes them for the rest of their lives, building firm foundations of wholesome qualities, and developing the gifts they have within them that will take them into the world. Our "mission field" can be the place we go to work, Monday to Friday, nine to five, regardless of if we have a vocation, or if we, "just have a job." However we spend our day, we can influence those around us.

I currently work as a mental health social worker/care coordinator in a community mental health team in Wales. I have one client who calls me his "little English rose," and another who often thanks me for the visits I make to him. I see a Christian lady who believes that God has brought me to her. These comments help me to believe I am in the place I am meant to be at this time. It provides me with a sense that I am actually helping others and being a support to them. Even when it appears I am not wanted, I have a sense that in doing what I can, I am of benefit. I worked with a lady for just over a year, and she really did not want me there. When she was well enough, I discharged her from the service. Within a month, she phoned the office to request I come back.

The feeling of not being wanted was especially evident when I worked in statutory child protection services. Part of my job was to investigate abuse alongside the police. No parent was happy to see us. There was the fear that I would take away their children, and should the concerns be high enough, I did. In undertaking assessments that safeguard children, the social worker in that context is often hated. But when you work to see that no child comes to significant harm, you have to tackle with complex situations and make hard decisions. The well-being of the child is of paramount importance. You do not get thanked. However, you do get a sense that you play a part improving the quality of a child's life.

PROJECTS

Having a project is always a good way to go. Projects can be large or small. To have a goal that is defined and achievable, and has a beginning and an end, can be accomplished by us all. To have a plan and see it come together allows us to wonder at its success. When we plan and have a project, we are able to move forward step by step. When we plan, we hope for the best. Many also plan for the worst-case scenario. In carrying out our plans, it is occasionally the case that we are left shocked and surprised. A good plan is not always a perfect plan. When shooting our arrow at the target, it is sometimes the case that we miss.

Fear of failure can be a huge barrier for us in moving forward. We should not see our failure as a disaster. Failure is an opportunity to start again, but this time, learning from the past mistakes. When you fail, the positive aspect is that you have learnt something. You have learnt how not to do it, what does not work. In failure, we have the opportunity to try a new approach. We can be encouraged to embrace a quality called perseverance. Many great people, many great achievements, experienced multiple failures before they triumphed.

No matter what the project is, it can make a difference to someone's life. It can have influence that comes to bear on others. Our actions can inspire those around us. Imagination, creativity, wisdom, focus, lead us to the fulfilment of the vision. Knowledge is not the be-all and end-all. It is often the case that the more I know, the less I know. Imagination, inspiration, determination, dedication go far. Vision may be invisible to others, but we do not see visions through our natural eyes. We need to be brave in bringing about that which is unseen into being seen. In connecting with others, we can help them get in touch with not only identifying but motivating them to actively embrace their own aspirations. When alive, our vision is contagious.

On one aid-giving project, I learnt the lesson of calculating what you need to take and what you don't need to take. This lesson also caused us to stop and think about where it might not be safe to take a white person. We had set aside one morning where we were going to a small fishing village to distribute food aid. We set up in an empty house, then opened the doors for people to come and collect supplies. It was predominantly the women who came forward to receive the goods, filling their bags with essentials. The men gathered in groups outside, watching. When it was time for us to go, we still had a number of items that needed to be packed up and put back in the truck to go to the next place. Realising we had more, the locals started demanding more to be given to them. As the only white person present, I became the focus of their desperation and want. I think because I was the white face, they thought I was in charge or something. I wasn't, but I stuck out in a crowd. The team closed the doors and started to pack up. The people remained outside, and the crowd did not disperse and go home. We needed an exit plan. After a while, my colleagues decided it might help if I were to leave. However, the question of how to get me out was not so straightforward. There was an angry mob outside, with machetes held high. Some of my colleagues formed a circle around me. We walked through the middle of the shouting, machete-wielding crowd with a certain element of haste, and I was bundled into the van. The van sped off, doing wheel spins as it went. It was definitely an occasion for lessons to be learnt!

CHURCH PLANTING

For those of you who do not move in church circles, church planting is, in short, starting a new church. Church isn't about a building, it's about a group of people. There are many different forms that church planting can take. Equally, there are many different styles that characterise a church. For me, the most important thing is that it should be culturally relevant. A new church, in a new area, should reflect and be shaped by the community it is established in. It should relate to those who live in the community and enhance the life of that community. Naturally, what works in one place does not necessarily work elsewhere. A style is not important. What is important is the shared ethos and values. I believe it is also important that a church does not become a club that only attends to its members.

A church should be encouraged to look outwards, minister to the wider community, and have a strong focus and vision. Organic, spontaneous growth is rich in quality and character. As it brings new life to itself, it also brings new life and goodness into the community. Allowing this organic growth can be a challenge to those who are involved in the planting process. We all have our own ideas of what a church should look like. There are things that we like and dislike, especially when it comes to style. Our own ideas, attitudes, and cultural background can get in the way of the new thing God is doing. Our hearts must be open. Pioneering comes with learning on the job, and it involves risk. When something is new and maybe even different, there will be obstacles in the way, but those with a courageous heart will overcome. A pioneer always has to make sacrifices along the way. They often forge a path that has not been travelled down before. Pioneers can be misunderstood. Some who are trying to be kind may say, "You are ahead of your time." But know that you were born for such a time as this! Do not be afraid of the wilderness as many a great thing has come out of a desert experience. To trail blaze may not be comfortable; it may even be painful. Imagine the case whereby we do not walk out of the wilderness but the wilderness itself springs to life. Streams and rivers begin to flow. Shoots of new life rise up out of the once barren and dry land. The landscape is transformed! Maybe our prayer should not be "God, get me out of here!" but "God, let me see your goodness, your life, in this desperate, hot, dark place." Our pioneering spirit may lead us to camp out at the gates of hell, and in my opinion, there is nothing wrong with that!

I have seen three new churches come about through my ministry years. One was a result of my evangelistic endeavours in Africa. This church was planted following a week of evangelistic meetings held in the open air. Other than the person appointed to be the pastor, all were new converts from those gatherings.

Another experience was the forming of a youth church here in Wales. This was a church of the unchurched. We started with a handful of youth, and within a year, we grew to be a church of one hundred young people from the local community. It was a case where they belonged before they believed. This was an interesting dynamic in itself. My third experience was the church in Hikkaduwa, Sri Lanka. This church came about through community interactions on a personal level and through community development. There have been some who have joined us from other churches, but this has been because there was now the opportunity to go to church in the area where they lived. However, the majority have been new believers. Three experiences, all different, but all culturally relevant.

The church in Hikkaduwa is where I found my strongest personal connection, but not because it reflects my style, as it so does not. I guess it is because it was where I invested a lot of time and energy. Hikkaduwa is a small coastal town very much on the tourist map. It is known for the good surf and attracts surfers from all over the world. It is also great for snorkelling and scuba diving. Sea turtles are regular visitors, as well as the many forms of sea life that congregate around the coral reef. It has mainstream hotels for the package tourist type. It is popular with travellers, with its many guest houses and cafés. The road, the main strip, runs parallel with the sea. It is lined with small huts selling all that Sri Lanka has to offer. The locals live on the many lanes and tracks that run off from the strip on the "jungle side." Hikkaduwa, however, also has a dark side. In addition to being flooded with drugs, it is also on the "Asian Triangle" of places to go for those that like to have sex with children. Children, even babies, are cheap in Hikkaduwa. There is a saying in Hikkaduwa: "Bon bons for the babies." That's how cheap the life of children are. There are parents that pimp their children out for what money they can get.

We lived jungle side, with the local people; this was our first step. Following that, we purchased push bikes and cycled around the neighbourhood saying hello to those we passed. We cycled the same route day after day, seeing the same people. There were times when we stopped to talk to them as our faces became familiar. What was interesting was that, after some time, we met people who we didn't recognise, but they seemed to know us. They stopped to talk to us. They had been observing us. They even said, "You are not like the other white people who come here. You do not get drunk or take drugs. You do not buy our children. You are good people." Without our realising it, our lifestyle and our actions had been noted and were speaking volumes.

By chance, or as some would like to say by "divine appointment," we met a local man in another town further down south. He had a heart for Hikkaduwa and wanted to start a church there. He also had a friendship with a man who ran a drug rehabilitation centre. We spent time with them, getting to know them, and shared dreams and visions for Hikkaduwa. What was significant about Hikkaduwa was that there was no church there at that time. In coming to know these two men we were provided with: 1) a route into the community, insofar as our home became a bit of a halfway house for locals who were addicted to drugs and 2) a future pastor.

We kept cycling and kept praying as we went. We also had an open house, keeping the front door open for anyone to come in at any time of the day, just like our neighbours did. One teenager used to come in on a regular basis. We had a local game, a Carrom board, which seemed to attract him in. One day he came over instead of going to school. We sent him away saying, "No school, no Carrom." That went down well with his family, even if he didn't like it. But he came back the next day telling us he had been to school and asking if he could now play. You see, when you live in a little community like that, each household has something that the other households do not have, and so those things are shared. Other than the Carrom board, we had the washing well in our back yard and a king coconut tree out front. The house opposite had a TV. When a curfew was on, we gathered in their living room for an evening to watch the news. One time, we saw a rat run around the top of the wall (their houses did not have ceilings, just the walls and the roof), soon followed by a rather large snake chasing after it. No one even batted an eyelid, because it was the norm! The house just up on the other side of the lane had the drinking well. Next door had the radio which blasted out monks chanting twice a day. Everyone had something to contribute.

After we had four people interested, we started to meet at our house on Sunday mornings. The meeting took the form of a talk, discussion, questions and answers, and prayer. Over the months, others came along, and the meetings started to grow. Unfortunately, we had to leave as we were unable to get resident visas. The work, however, carried on. I would fly back and forth on a regular basis in the early years, bring encouragement and teachings. Twenty-six years on, they are a group of 100-plus people meeting in central Hikkaduwa. But that's not it. They have planted churches in many villages and towns all over that region. Over the years, they have grown, developed, and reproduced multiple times over. It has taken on a life of its own. What is great is that it has had nothing to do with me, and that is so cool!

THE PERSECUTED CHURCH

Christians all over the world have been—and continue today to be—persecuted for their faith and belief. In recent years, this has been highlighted by the plight of Christians in Iraq. When ISIS moved into the north of the country, they painted the Arabic letter "N" on the homes of Christians and their churches. Why "N"? To be labelled with an "N" stood for "Nazarenes," referring to people believed to follow Jesus of Nazareth, rather than Islam. If a household had the letter "N" painted on the wall, and the occupants did not make a public conversion to Islam, they were faced with one of two choices—leave without any material possessions or die. Any person who chose to be "N" paid a high price. The cost was great. Christian pastors were dragged out in front of their communities and families and were beheaded. Even children of Christian families were shot dead.

Christians in some African countries, and other places on the globe such as Pakistan, Sri Lanka, Malaysia, Mozambique, Indonesia, China, North Korea, Iran, Peru, Russia, to name a few, are imprisoned, forced into slavery, beaten, tortured, raped, killed. They endure much suffering and sacrifice. Many stand strong amidst such horrors, full of faith.

The church I was involved in planting in Sri Lanka has faced, and continues to face, persecution from the Buddhist majority. Many find this hard to believe, as Buddhism is seen as peaceful and "no Buddhist would harm a fly." However, I know from first-hand experience that the truth is, there are Buddhist monks who stir a crowd into mob mentality and incite violence against Christians and the church. In Sri Lanka, it is not only the Christians who have seen persecution but also the Muslims. In a shared persecution, Christians and Muslims have supported one another.

The church in Hikkaduwa had been attacked on a Sunday morning as they gathered together to worship. One morning, a large mob led by

Buddhist monks stormed the church. They beat up the pastor, threatened to rape the women, and burned Bibles. At this time, we were renting a building to meet in. The landlord, although sympathetic, withdrew from the agreement, and we were left without a meeting place. No other landlord would rent to us either, due to the fear that their property would be burned down. The church in Hikkaduwa had no option other than to meet in another town which was fourteen miles down the road. We transported members in the back of a truck to the living room of someone's house. We did lose a few members due to fear. When we were able to get back into Hikkaduwa, we were in the position where we were able to buy our own place by the railway line. When we returned, we were faced with another attack. A large crowd led by monks descended on the church. They trashed the place, leaving glass and paint everywhere. As they stormed through the front door, the men ushered the women and children out the back door. Neighbours took them into their houses and hid them. We are now in a position that, if they burn us down, we will just rebuild.

In the early days, when we were small, we used to meet in the front room of the house where my husband and I lived. One evening, a crowd of about 200 people, led by a few monks, came down the lane and gathered outside our home. Many were carrying torches and they were shouting. Three neighbours, who were not members of our little church, stepped forward and spoke to the crowd. One was a teenager, another an old lady, and the third, the wife of a drug addict. Culturally speaking, these three people had little significance and standing. One by one, they addressed the crowd. They said that my husband and I were good people, that we were here to help, and they testified to our character and good works. Each gave personal testimony of how we had helped them. When they spoke, a silence came over the people gathered, and the atmosphere changed. People started to drop their torches, and the crowd dispersed. The monks looked around to find they were standing there on their own, and so they too left. They never came to our home again in such a manner.

HUMANITARIAN RESPONSE IN TIMES OF DISASTER

A "disaster" is defined by www.dictionary.com as "a calamitous event, especially one occurring suddenly and causing great loss of life, damage, or hardship." The International Strategy for Disaster Reduction (UNISDR) provides this definition: "A disaster is a function of the risk process. It results from the combination of hazards, conditions of vulnerability, and insufficient capacity or measures to reduce the potential negative consequences of risk."

All disasters bring with them an immense effect upon individuals, families, communities, regions, nations, and even the international community. The results have been the loss of human life, the changing shape of communities, and an increase in global awareness. The effects of disasters upon communities deemed to be vulnerable are immense. From a social perspective, for me, exploring approaches of vulnerability, well-being, and participation as a means of intervention has been crucial.

The definition of "humanitarianism" by www.dictionary.com is "having a concern for or helping to improve the welfare and happiness of people, pertaining to the saving of human lives and the alleviation of suffering."

The humanitarian sector is underpinned by codes and standards, values and ethics, policies and legislation. You will also find that there is guidance and principles for internally displaced persons (IDPs) and for children in the United Nations Convention on the Rights of the Child (UNCRC). Examples include situations where some countries have taken on-board and ratified those, where other countries have not. In cases where countries have not, it can be somewhat frustrating for the worker.

There are a number of themes catalogued in the field of disaster studies. Terms, theories, and methods of intervention are to be understood. It is good to be familiar with them. These three shape the response given by those who venture out into the risky environments where they seek to serve. They can be identified in the following terms:

- Prevention
- Mitigation
- Preparedness
- Risk
- Response or disaster relief
- Rehabilitation
- Recovery

Theories are also used to identify intervention types.

- Family-centred perspective
- Integrated model
- Vulnerability
- Risk reduction—Pressure and Release Model (PAR), the Access Model
- Psychosocial theory
- Solidarity theory
- International political theory

And there are other methods of intervention.

- Traditional approaches
- Community-based therapeutic care (CTC)
- Whole community development
- Intervention wheel/program spiral
- The cluster approach

After the Asian tsunami in 2005, the Inter-Agency Standing Committee (IASC) conducted a review of humanitarian response. It looked at ways to improve emergency response in making adjustments through lessons learnt from the Asian tsunami, and the natural disasters in Haiti and Pakistan. This review led to a working principle of "the cluster approach." Each "cluster" established normally has a lead organisation at its centre providing information and management. It is encircled by numerous sectors of response.

These sectors include health, water supply, sanitation and hygiene promotion (WASH), emergency shelter, camp management and coordination, food security, nutrition, protection, education, emergency telecommunications, early recovery, and logistics. Since then, to strengthen the whole system, updates to protocols have been implemented in strengthening leadership, increasing stakeholder accountability, and improving coordination.

When out in the field, regardless of the role performed, there is a mutual aim and thrust to the work and labour that crosses and joins together those people. "The goals of intervention after any disaster are to decrease immediate trauma and the chances of long-term damage; to decrease the time it takes for people to recover; and to facilitate recovery by enhancing ways of coping, and by decreasing risk factors" (Rosenfeld, Caye, Ayalon & Lahad, 2005).

It can be seen that, for these goals to be achieved, agencies engage in interventions of "response" and "recovery." The immediate and short-term mobilization of resources to protect life, and mechanisms for intermediate and long-term efforts to stabilise and restore functionality to communities by methods of reconstruction and sustainable development, are adopted by the humanitarian worker.

"Social work" is concerned with the promotion of welfare with individuals, families, groups, and communities. Firstly, disaster studies very much deals with social issues and working with people. This is achieved by valuing and empowering others and providing services that support and enable, regardless of one's ethnic background, gender, age, religion, and class or caste. Presented to those who engage in humanitarian work are strong overtones that encourages anti-discriminatory and anti-oppressive practice. Values and interventions exult the worker to operate with high regard for others, and to be culturally sensitive and non-judgemental of people and their situations.

There is the suggestion that, over time, professional approaches which focus on poverty, deprivation, and injustice, in seeking to bring about social change by the means of social development in the third world, have steered policies and practice.

Children are an extremely vulnerable group when catastrophe strikes. In stating the obvious, children are smaller and have less physical strength than that of an adult. Likewise, a child's immune system is more sensitive and still developing, compared to the built-up immunities already acquired by an adult. This makes children more prone to contract diseases before adults, and less resilient in fighting off that disease. Despite generalised observations on the difference between adults and children, there arguably remains a case where some children are more vulnerable than others. They can also be at risk of exploitation. In working with children post-disaster, consideration is not only to be given to their vulnerability but also the child's well-being, the child's rights, and the participation that children can bring into the situation to shape their own lives.

The theory of vulnerability is broad, but despite the all-encompassing nature of vulnerability in times of disaster, there appear to be those who slip through the vulnerability net—those who are more at risk, more open to extreme forms of abuse, and more exposed to elements that threaten their very survival. Vulnerability is not only a condition caused by disasters but is also present in society even before a disaster strikes. Social divisions that set apart the elderly, the disabled, children, and the poor from mainstream society existed prior to the disaster. However, during a disaster and in the aftermath of it, these already vulnerable groups become more vulnerable than the "mainstream" who themselves have just been made vulnerable. It is fair to say that the participation of children in times of disaster is a hotly debated one when it comes to adults. Children themselves believe their voices should be heard and that they have a role to play in 'creating a new future for communities that rise from the rubble of ruin.' Community development as a means of participation by children and young people can be suggested, in an attempt to affect the grassroots of building or rebuilding communities in response to disaster situations.

The community plays a strong role in its own disaster interventions. Community development provides an holistic approach which is sustainable and focuses on the community's interests rather than those of donors, agencies, or any other outside force. Community development empowers its members to meet their own needs with help and support available to be drawn upon. In overlaying a paradigm of community development in tackling vulnerable children, the wider and larger issues of environment, economics, and politics go beyond family, friends, workplace, school, etc., and into the realms of social policy and social planning for change.

Navigating your way through a disaster is not always easy. It can be very challenging and draining on the human soul. The work seems endless at times. The task at hand is often massive. It is important that the worker does not become part of the problem, ending up as just another mouth to feed. The rewards, however, can be phenomenal. Being involved in seeing dramatic change has a positive outcome and can fill your heart with joy.

THE ASIAN TSUNAMI

On the 26th December, 2004, Boxing Day morning. The tsunami struck the coast of Sri Lanka and other Asian countries. The wave surge swept the eastern coastline of Sri Lanka, destroying shorefronts up to a kilometre inland. The tsunami curled around the southern and northern coasts, causing damage along these heavily populated areas. Twelve out of the twenty-five districts of Sri Lanka were severely damaged. According to the United Nations High Commission of Refugees (UNHCR) in Colombo, the total number of deaths caused by the tsunami in Sri Lanka were 31,225, internally displaced persons (IDPs) 518,698, and missing persons 4,101.

On 26th December 2004, I was in Disneyland Paris. News of the disaster started to filter through the news channels. People I knew and loved were in the reported disaster zone. Returning home the following day, I found I was unable to make contact with my people in Hikkaduwa and Galle. All communications were down. Information being broadcast through the media was not positive. Death, destruction, disease, civil unrest, and the fear of a second wave flooded our TV screens. I felt compelled to go and be with the folks I knew. I wanted to assist them in any way I could. Through my connections at home, people donated toward the relief effort. The outpouring of response was staggering. Local hospitals donated medical supplies. Asda, the supermarket where I was chaplain, also donated much. A camping shop somehow got in touch with me and donated five large family tents. This was just the start of institutions, churches, businesses, and individuals giving what they had, through us. More came in over the coming weeks.

I can remember the conversation I had with my husband. We decided only one of us should go, initially, just in case he or she didn't come back. The conversation went that our daughter needed one of us to bring her up and be there for her as a parent. We decided I was to go. For the first time ever, I was nervous when I boarded the plane. When the doors shut, I thought, *That's it, there is no going back.* I was committed to the mission at hand. The plane held the donated items of relief and aid that I somehow got through baggage checks without having to pay extra charges. On 1st January 2005, I arrived in Sri Lanka.

The journey from Colombo down south to Galle was a very long one. Roads that were on the normal route had been washed away, and we therefore had to find another way, using the back roads and tracks. On my arrival, I discovered that, by a miracle, all the members of our church were alive. However, a number of them had lost everything—houses, possessions, businesses. What was remarkable, and a testimony to their resilience and character, was that they had already started to help others. Together we made plans of how we would assist not only members of our own church but also people in the wider community. And so, the story of aid, relief, recovery, and development continued and snowballed.

MY BIGGEST REGRET

In my experience, a missionary life for a Brit is not an easy life. It is often one of poverty. However, in that poverty, I have known riches. Riches not as the world sees, in wealth and luxury, but riches in the blessings. When I was in the mission organisation, we did not get paid, we did not have a wage or salary, we had to pay our own way, we were not helped out with flights, accommodation, food, or any projects we undertook, and this was even less so when I operated independently. It was called "living by faith." Yes, we had our own sponsors, and from time to time, we received gifts from others, but the extent of this funding never reached the level whereby it even qualified us to pay taxes. During one particularly lean period, I was praying for food. Unbelievably, a joint of meat was left on my back doorstep. It was amazing to receive such a gift. I have no idea to this day who sneaked into my garden and left it there for me to cook up and enjoy. There were times when I would have been better off had I been living off state benefits. There were times when I looked at the others on the mission field, like the Americans and South Koreans, and I was jealous of the resources available to them. Equally, those who worked for large international organisations who were well provided for, both personally and in the work they undertook. I never experienced hotel living, fine dining, air-conditioned offices and apartments, luxury travel, or finances for large scale projects. I lived with the local people in their differing forms of accommodation, and if there was no accommodation, I slept under the stars. I ate what they ate. I washed with other women at the well or by the river side. This style of living, however, had many benefits. Firstly, it created a connection between me and the people I had gone to serve. When I first went to wash with the women at the well, they were initially taken aback and amused by the situation, as "the whites" did not normally do this. However, it formed a bond and oneness between us all. Despite these benefits, the lack of financial backing was at times difficult, and I knew that if I had the resources, I could have done so much more.

My biggest regret was not something I did, but something I did not do, something I was unable to do, as I was not in the position to do it. It is something I often think about, and I don't want to be in a position again that, when asked for help, I am unable to meet the need and give. However, the more I have reflected on the situation, the more I have tried to console myself that we cannot be the answer to every incident that presents itself before us. There is a wisdom in knowing when the job at hand is for someone bigger and better than yourself.

Post-tsunami, I visited a village in the northeast of Sri Lanka. It was a remote cut-off community. Their coastal village was located in Tamil Tiger (LTTE) territory. This village was a vulnerable community for a number of reasons.

1) They were a Muslim community living in a Tamil Tiger area.

2) It was reported that the LTTE were recruiting child soldiers in the wake of the tsunami. I had read in one of the national newspapers that UNICEF had received information that more than sixty cases of child conscription into the LTTE during the first eight weeks after the tsunami occurred, which was believed to be only a quarter of the actual number of children conscripted.

3) I was also told by my sources in the United Nations, World Food Programme (WFP), and Médecines sans Frontieres that access to the East had initially been blocked by the Sri Lankan military. No agencies were permitted into the disaster zone unless they were willing to pay a heavy bribe in order to get aid trucks through. It was the case that humanitarian aid workers had not yet reached this community.

4) There was a risk to aid workers in going there. I had already helped to evacuate colleagues from the organisation World Vision (a different organisation to the one I worked for) from a bomb threat they received a couple of weeks earlier in a different location. Aid workers can be a vulnerable group themselves. Risks to humanitarian staff and missionaries, for that matter, include threats and occurrences of assault, sniper fire, rape, abduction, angry mobs, and death, just to name a few.

5) There was a small window when going to visit with the community. I had to drive through a minefield to get to them on a single dirt track; I had to leave by a certain time in the afternoon as the elephants use that track in the evenings in getting to wherever they

wanted to go. You don't mess with an elephant making its passage through a minefield!

Due to the lack of assistance, this community was way behind in receiving relief efforts, efforts other parts of the country were benefiting from. I arrived at this village three months after the disaster struck. It was my observation that people were still in shock. Men were sitting around looking at the debris, not knowing where to start. I set my team to work with the children, engaging in psycho-social play, drawing on resources provided by parachute games, and singing. The women also gathered, and this provided an opportunity for me to talk with them. Although value can be attributed to this form of engagement, I was left knowing there was a much bigger picture that was in need of attention. While my team were doing this, I was invited to walk and talk with the village elders. They showed me the devastation that had ripped through their community. Prior to my visit, I had been asked by a Muslim non-governmental organisation (NGO) based on the west coast, north of Colombo, to monitor and evaluate the relief progress. I had the opportunity to hear from the community leaders. The head elder was asking for complete community development and change that affected the children, the women, the men, their community place of meeting, their housing, and their livelihoods. They had lost everything. That man turned to me and begged me to come and live with them in their community, to set up community development, to rebuild their village. He said, "Whatever you say for us to do, I will see that we all do it." I was somewhat taken aback and shocked at this. A Muslim man, the head elder, had asked me, a Christian woman, to do this. I guess this was evidence of his degree of desperation. His face, his words, haunt me to this day. I was not able to fulfil his request, even though I would have loved to do so, and I wanted to be able to shake his hand and say, "Yes."

Despite my regret of not being able to assist in this project myself, I handed over my report to another organisation to assist them in rebuilding. I felt this would result in the best outcome for them as a community.

A little bit of faith

CHAPTER EIGHT
GO!

"History is supposed to be different, because I am alive."

Laura Ruth

THE MISSIONARY CALLING

I have already mentioned a number of areas of operations that I have encountered on the mission field, but for you Christians reading this, there are matters of the heart that need to be addressed. Additionally, there is the question of "What is a missionary?" and "Where am I called?" When this question is asked, some may give the name of a country as response. Others will give a type of function. As I was twenty years in what we would traditionally recognise as the "full-time ministry," it would be remiss of me not to share with you some structure and framework on this.

My traditional missionary days may be identified by some as *in the past*, but in my heart, I am still a missionary. I believe in everything I am doing, I am a missionary. Therefore, I have been a missionary for thirty-five years, the past fifteen years here in Wales. Maybe in the future, God will again propel me and I will go out once again into the far flung nations, but if not, that's okay, as I am moving in a role of bringing long-term lasting transformation to the culture where I am placed.

Endurance

Breakthrough

Let us start here. In order to be a missionary, you must know—it is not a job. To be a missionary is a lifestyle. It is a life of developing intimacy with God, devotion to Him.

THE GREAT COMMISSION

After Jesus was raised from the dead, he spent time with his disciples before ascending to heaven. Jesus told them to "Go into all the world" (Matthew 28:17-20). This was not just a great idea on His part, it was a command. Not only did he tell them to go, but he also instructed them on what to do when they went. In the going, Jesus tells us in the great commission, to "go and make disciples, baptise them, teach them." Why? "Because He has been given all authority in heaven and on earth." And as far as we are concerned, we are to be confident in the knowledge that "He is with us always, even to the end of the age."

We are sent out to change the world. Tell yourself that history is supposed to be different because I am alive. There really isn't an excuse not to go, to write history, change the world, and shake up nations. In fact, anything less than world change is a compromise. There are some who may be afraid of what God may ask of them to do, or where God may ask them to go. There are some who may not feel equipped. Some may come up with a hundred reasons for why they should not go. Life circumstances may be difficult. You may say, "I can't afford it. Where does the money come from?"

When Jesus met on that mountain with His disciples, where He imparted what we know as the "Great Commission," Matthew 28:17 says, "When they saw Him, they worshiped Him; but some were doubtful." What I find amazing here is that Jesus gave the command for them to go into all the world—to the doubters among them as well. So, in Jesus' book, even if you fall into the category of being a doubter as a disciple of His, you are still qualified to go!

Matthew 6:33 tells us to "seek first the kingdom of God and His righteousness and all these things will be added unto you." In the runup to Jesus telling us to "seek first His kingdom," He encourages us "not to worry, don't be anxious." We are not to worry about what and when we may eat, how we are going to clothe ourselves, where we are going to live and so on. God will provide.

This is easy to say. When your calling and faith is, let's say, emotionally strong, yes, you believe that with all your heart. Speaking from my own experience, as time goes on, that can be so difficult. Faith does not come from an emotional strength. Faith is a deep knowing, a deep trust.

I have known times when this type of faith in the provision of God has been seriously tested. It is when you don't have any money to buy food for your next meal, let alone anything else. I have looked around me at others, and I confess I have been jealous of their seemingly abundance—in the high level of financial support they receive, some from millionaire backers, some being sent out from large, rich churches. I look and my heart sinks as I pick up pennies off the floor, dropped by others, so I gather these pennies to buy a loaf of bread. There was even a day when I was given a few cans of soup where I cried, not just because I was thankful but because it was the best food source I had received for some time.

I've prayed, "Lord, these shoes have holes in them. Is there any chance of a new pair, please?" There was even a time where I envied people living off benefits from the government, because they were better off than me. Faith in God being the God of provision was majorly tested. It's hard. But, we are not to confuse the goodness of God with our own comfort. I would even go as far as to say as a missionary that the greatest challenge to our faith is not persecution. It is struggles we encounter when we need to believe in Him for food, clothes, a roof over our head.

Our response is important. Jesus said, "Repent and believe." My heart was not right with God. God will always provide for His vision. It may not look like what we have imagined. It may not be as we were hoping for. It may not fit with our carefully devised plans.

We may have had in mind that to do our work, we require a lovely air conditioned 4x4 Jeep. Then God provides us with a bicycle. He has still provided! But I do know this: if I had that Jeep rather than the push bike, I wouldn't have stopped off to speak with the locals as they waved and called us over. The opportunity to begin to make friends and tell them about Jesus as I pedalled around the villages might not have even happened. In that Jeep, I would have driven right past them.

SURRENDER

God requires of us radical obedience to Him. Every day we must surrender to Him and His will. Jesus says in John 14:15, "If you love Me, you will keep My commandments." What are His commandments? They are found in Luke 10:27: "You shall love the Lord your God with all your heart, and with all your soul, and all your strength, and with all your mind; and your neighbour as yourself." We are to totally immerse ourselves with every fibre of our being in our love for God himself. This is the first commandment. This is our first calling. Everything we do must flow from a place of intimacy.

It is like Jesus is saying, "Look into my eyes, you will see what you mean to Me." Our response: "Search my heart, search my soul. Take me as I am, take my life. I would give it all. There's no love like your love. And no one could give more love. There's nowhere unless you're there. Everything I do, I do it for you: walk the wire for you. I'd die for you. I'm going all the way. And we'll see it through. Everything I do, I do it for you."

This a love song, as it happens, not from the Bible. These are the lyrics found in a song from Bryan Adams in his 1991 hit. It was number one in the UK charts for sixteen weeks. It was a song played at many a wedding party at that time. It struck me that this depth of passion is what it is like in having Jesus as our first love. It also struck me that the world is crying out for this depth of love and passion. Why else would it top the charts for so long? People want it so desperately. Where else will they truly find it other than in Him?

In the context as serving in the nations as a missionary, it is this: "Everything I do, I do it for you." To the point that I'd "walk the wire for you, I'd die for you." The passion and depth of love in our hearts for Jesus is to be this strong. Nothing else will do. When we interact with and give to others, it must be from a place of love. If we do not have love, we have nothing, we are nothing (1 Corinthians 13).

How do you cultivate this strength of love to the point of total surrender? Simply by spending time with Him. How do you do that? Firstly, by reading the Bible. The Bible reveals Jesus to us. That's how we know Him. Secondly, in prayer. Have a good old chat with Him. Whisper sweet nothings in His ear. Express your love for Him. It's a place of intimacy. If you do not have the words to express what is in your heart, speak in your heavenly tongue. Listen to Him. Prayer is not a monologue. It's a two-way conversation. In prayer, relationship is developed. Third, worship Him, "in spirit and in truth" (John 4:24). Let your love songs flow. Exalt Him. Why? Because He is worthy. Yes, I'm going to say that again. He is worthy.

WEAKNESS

When we are in that place of total surrender, we see the glory of God. We marvel at how amazing He is. We are also humbled. We become very aware of our own failings, weaknesses, inadequacies. A place of weakness is a good thing, a good place to be as long as you don't start having a pity party. Jesus says, "apart from Me, you can do nothing" (John 15:5).

In 2 Corinthians 12:9, it says, "And He said to them, My grace is sufficient for you, for power is perfected in weakness. Most gladly, therefore, I will rather boast about my weaknesses, so the power of Christ may dwell in me." The apostle Paul, a missionary, knew this. When he needed to defend his apostleship, he did not boast of the miracles he had performed but rather of his weaknesses. His loss and his suffering were his qualifications. This is not the way of the world. The world seeks qualifications in amazing achievements. That is not the kingdom way. Paul spoke as a "fool." He had been in prison, was flogged, exposed to death, stoned, shipwrecked, in danger from rivers, in danger from bandits, in danger wherever he went, had gone without sleep, without food, was cold and naked, and was weak.

He boasted in his weakness (2 Corinthians 11:16-33). Now, that's what I call a great advert for the call to be a missionary!

I know I am weak. My weaknesses stick out like a sore thumb. Is it wise to send out a missionary who is a schizophrenic with manic depression, and all the baggage that comes with that? There are many who would say no. However, when you shine the light of the heart of the gospel over it, it sounds like a possible "good" qualification. I may be considered as too risky and therefore disqualified from being sent out by others to the nations. But, other than Jesus Himself, every character in the Bible was risky. They all had their issues, but God chose them and anointed them. God chose risky people and put them into risky situations. With their success, it only goes to highlight how great God is and not how great that person was. It is all to the glory of God.

Taking risks are for those who, for the cause of the gospel, seek to make a lasting difference by faith. Risks are being willing to live or die for the gospel. Esther said, "If I perish, I perish" (Esther 4:16). Esther did not know in advance what the outcomes of her actions would be. On the far side of every risk—even if it results in death—the love of God triumphs. John the Baptist risked, and he got his head chopped off. Paul risked, and we know what happened to him; his list of woes was as long as my arm.

It seems to me that faith and risk often go hand in hand. Hebrews 11 reminds us of Bible greats who, by faith, obeyed and risked all. In my experience, little though it is, the word "obedience" often can be translated as the word "risk." Paul writes in Philippians 4:12, "I can do all things through Him who strengthens me." All things—in all the crap, in all my weaknesses—in all trials, He will give me strength.

A SERVANT'S HEART

There is a place of power in our weaknesses. God is also close to the broken-hearted (Psalm 34:18). When we arrive on our mission field, there should be no fanfare that says, "I have arrived, I am here." We are there to serve. We are to serve with joy. No one wants to see a miserable missionary. Get your heart right. We are not there to build our own ministry. We firstly serve our master, King Jesus. Radical obedience, radical servanthood, requires us to give our lives away in the midst of all the chaos that surrounds us. What God does and how He does it is up to Him. It is not about putting our own name on the map. In everything we do, however we serve, it is His name that is glorified.

WE ARE THE SUPERNATURAL PEOPLE OF GOD

In the context of missions, as believers we have an added a "bit of spice" to our endeavours of seeing global change. The good news of Jesus crosses all cultural boundaries. As missionaries, we are also commissioned to demonstrate the power of His Kingdom, in seeing it spread far and wide. It is not enough to simply talk about it. We are empowered by God's spirit in signs and wonders.

Acts 1:8 states, ". . . you will receive power when the Holy Spirit has come upon you; and you shall be My witnesses both in Jerusalem, and in all Judea and Samaria, and even to the remotest part of the earth." These are the words of Jesus. Here He provides a direct link between the supernatural and missions. It was the intention of God that the evidence of His supernatural power be deployed as we give witness to Him in all the earth. With every step that we move forward, the kingdom of God is advanced as we operate in a naturally supernatural way. It is this that makes the difference. Demonstrations of His power are meant to be for the world—out there in the open. They are not just meant to be stuck within the secrecy of the four walls that we call our church.

Healings, deliverance, dreams, visions, hearing His voice, angelic encounters, slaying dragons, going up into the third heaven, miracles, power over the forces of nature, powerful encounters with a living God, displays of His Spirit at work—all are to accompany us on the mission field. Manifestations, visitations of God, outpourings of His Spirit transform others and yields fruit.

It all starts with our own intimate experience in our relationship with God. I live ten minutes down the road from where Evan Roberts lived, ten minutes from where the Welsh revival of 1904 started. Evan Roberts, the great revivalist, was a man who experienced great intimacy with God. It was said of Evan Roberts that every night for three months before the revival began, he was removed from his body into the third heaven from 1 a.m. to 5 a.m. Then from 9 a.m. to noon, away he would go up, out of this world, to spend time with Jesus himself. David Morgan, another Welsh revivalist of 1859, experienced heaven before the Lord propelled him back to earth to begin his revival ministry. This out-of-body experience is but a supernatural encounter; however, this encounter will bring heaven down on earth. This type of encounter so grips the revivalist that they rock the world.

In my young missionary days, I would pray as I lay on my bed at night, *God, is tonight the night?* A number of times in those days I would see a glimpse of heaven. I saw angel armies, I saw lights in the sky, I saw golden paths that led to golden archways, I saw more colours than could be mixed with a paintbrush, I would go up mountains, run alongside Jesus, go swimming in warm waters, and splash around with him, and we would laugh together.

In addition, there were visions and dreams that were so vivid. On one occasion back in the '80s, I saw Christians walking through cities, towns, and villages, declaring the name of Jesus. I saw believers walking from north to south all over the UK, from top to bottom. From John O'Groats to Lands' End. I shared this vision with the founder of our missionary organisation. I had written my vision down on paper and popped it into an envelope for him. He was part of a national group of leaders. He shared it with others. Within a year, we had the "March for Jesus" campaign here in the UK.

In looking back at the spiritual and supernatural encounters I have had over the years, it is the first occasions that I remember most: the first vision, the first healing, the first deliverance, the first time in heaven, the first prophetic word, the first time I preached to hundreds in Africa, the first church plant, and so on.

When I was seventeen years of age, I worked for a short period in an old people's home. My boss was unable to work one day; she could not walk because of her arthritis. She lived on site. At the end of my shift, I went to see her to enquire how she was and ask if she needed anything. She told me of the pain she was in. I asked if I could pray for her. She said "Yes," so I did. I started to pray for her healing. I prayed that the pain would leave her, and she would be able to walk okay. After a couple of minutes, I asked her how the pain was. I asked if she was able to move her foot. She informed me it was much better, but there was still some pain there. I replied, "Okay, we haven't finished yet, then. I'll pray some more." And so I prayed again. I then asked her if she could wiggle her foot. She did, and as she did, I started praying in tongues, my heavenly language. She laughed and so did I. But I kept praying. I paused and asked her again, how was the pain? She replied, "It's gone." We looked at the clock, and I had missed my bus. She offered to drive me home. As she drove her little car, using the clutch pedal, she looked down and smiled, then looked at me. She was in awe that she had been healed. I was then able to tell her about Jesus. She was healed before she was saved. I think there is something in that!

CALLING

Our biggest calling is to be like Jesus. You are not called to a country or to a type of ministry. When I joined the missionary organisation that I worked directly with for just over a decade, we met together daily to pray for the nations. These times of prayer were a launch pad in being sent out and going. If I asked of my fellow missionary, "What are you called to?" the answer would often come back as a name of a country or region. "I'm called to Morocco," or "I'm called to the Middle East."

Sometimes during our prayer meetings, someone would say, "All those called to Africa, gather in that part of the room to pray for those nations" or "All called to Asia, go into this area and pray." I would sit there and think, *I know I am a missionary, but am I the only one that does not feel called to a particular nation? Is it because I am only fifteen years old and God hasn't therefore given me a nation yet?* Then when I turned eighteen and was a full-time missionary, I wondered why I still could not say I am called to such a nation. I said to myself, *How can you have a missionary that is not called anywhere?*

I knew I had a heart for the nations, and I knew I was supposed to be a missionary, but where was I going? I just felt called to follow Jesus and to go to any nation He sent me. Wherever He sent me was cool with me. I really didn't mind; I would go anywhere He told me to go. This bothered me. I was the youngest person in that missionary organisation at that time. Was my lack of calling down to my youth? It was years later when I realised my heart was in the right place. My calling was indeed to follow Jesus with every part of me and to follow Him to the ends of the earth, wherever and whenever.

If I arrived in Africa for a short period of time, then I went off to South America, then Asia, that was okay. If I never settled in one particular nation, if I never fully immersed myself in that culture, if I never became fluent in that local language because I wasn't there long enough, then that was okay as long as I was following Jesus and going where He took me. Here I would like to say, if you are following Jesus to live in a particular nation, it is so important to spend time to master the national language.

At the time, I never felt like a real missionary. I looked at others around me and felt inadequate because I didn't give myself to one particular nation and because I wasn't fluent in another language. I had bits of different languages in my head, a few words and phrases in a number of languages. When I was somewhere that was not English-speaking, I would start a sentence in Sinhala, switch to French midway, and finish in Brazilian Portuguese without even realising it. My words were all mixed up. I still do that today. I was on a ward in our local psychiatric hospital and the psychiatrist was from Sri Lanka. I started the conversation in Sinhala. He responded in Sinhala, and I replied in Welsh. I knew I was speaking in a foreign language, but it wasn't until I got to my car that I realised what I had done. I felt so foolish.

And so, there is the problem. I looked around and compared myself to others, and thus my focus on Jesus was distracted. In doing that, I swallowed the lie that I was not a real missionary, when in fact, I was. I knew my calling but didn't feel I was good enough.

You are not called to a type of ministry. There are tools that we can deploy in the mission field. Humanitarian aid, community development, church planting, evangelism, and so on. There are many references in the Bible to ministering to the poor, the widows, and the orphans. There are references to feeding the hungry, among other practical things. Supernatural practises—winning souls for Christ, preaching the good news of the gospel, praying for the sick, casting out demons, even raising the dead—hold importance. The ability to operate in these functions are tools in our tool kit. I would suggest that they are not our primary calling.

To have knowledge and a skill base is fantastic. Your knowledge and skills along with your expertise, professional qualifications, and academic qualifications will all be of benefit, useful even, and I'm sure also deployed in the work that you do. But don't worry if you don't have them. The best type of training is on the job, in my opinion.

What is important is that you are humble and teachable. To be teachable is an attitude we should have. There is no place for "know-it-alls." To be teachable is different than to be trainable. If you are trainable, this will affect your actions—what you do and how you do it. To be teachable, this will affect your attitudes. Jesus Himself is the great teacher. We must learn from Him. When you are called to follow Him, when you are called to go out into the mission field, God has not chosen you because of the skills you already have.

In going to the nations, we must not impose our Western ideas, ways, and styles on the people we go to serve. We must not impose a Western image of Jesus on them.

In reality, when on the mission field, it is no different from being at home. Life is day-to-day. It's about having a balanced lifestyle. We established routines. Make friends. Go to the local market or shop to buy food. It is amazing how the price comes down when you at least attempt to speak the local language. We learn to cook with the equipment available. Another area that you need to learn to deal with is the toilet situation. Often a toilet is a hole in the ground. Creepy crawlies, spiders bigger than my hand, snakes, and cockroaches need to be dealt with. I was the one elected to remove them from our living quarters, and my main rule was, not in my bed—I drew a line there. It is also important to make sure you get enough sleep and have a bit of "me" time.

If you give your life to "the cause" and "the ministry," you will burn out. If you give your life to following Jesus afresh, each and every single day, you will indeed soar with eagles. "Yet those who wait on the Lord will gain new strength; They will mount up with wings like eagles, They will run and not get tired, They will walk and not become weary" (Isaiah 40:31).

From day one, when Jesus started to gather His disciples, he was upfront and clear about his intentions. He did not con his disciples. He did not sugar-coat what the cost would be. He was totally transparent. He simply said, "Follow Me, and I will make you fishers of men" (Matthew 4:19). A call to follow Him is a call to intimacy with Him. This is the first thing, the greatest thing of all. The calling of a missionary is to follow Him.

Second, to be fishers of men. In the natural world, being a fisherman is one of the hardest jobs there is. And it is so in the spiritual sense of being a fisher of men as well. It will be hard work. It is not for the faint-hearted. You need grit.

I have planned out what my ministry should look like so many times. I am now convinced that God laughs at all my plans. Great strategies and good ideas are nothing if they are not from God—and I thought I had a few great ones, but, no.

I say, rip up your own flow charts of what you are going to do and how you are going to do it. When you wake each morning, before your feet hit the ground, say "God, what today?" Then the devil will say, "Oh, no, she got out of bed! This could get seriously dangerous."

What about this for a prayer?

May all your expectations be frustrated,
May all your desires be dashed,
May all your plans be thwarted,
May all your hopes come to be withered into nothingness,
That you may experience the powerlessness and poverty of a child
And sing and dance in the love of God the Father, Son and Spirit.

—Brennan Manning

We are to be the face, hands, and feet of Jesus in this world. Have the courage to follow the Holy Spirit each and every moment of the day. Only go and do what He leads you into. There, you will be fruitful. There, life will flow.

I have asked of myself, *How do I know the will of God for my life?* I believe this is a common question among believers. I have been with the Lord for thirty-six years now. There are times when I really want to hear from God for guidance and direction. I so desperately want to hear what God is saying and what I should do, which path I should take. Sometimes I feel stuck. Sometimes I wish God would speak clearly and say, "Go here, go there, do this, do that." But there are times when he doesn't say anything. I cannot hear his voice. My next step is often to contact a couple of trusted Christian friends and ask them if they have a prophetic word for me. Then when they haven't, I ask if they have any thoughts on my dilemma and the choices ahead of me. Again, they often do not have any to offer in the way I was hoping for. It's great to receive prophetic words, but what do you do when you haven't got one?

Psalm 121:1-2 says, "I lift my eyes up to the mountains; from where shall my help come? My help comes from the Lord Who made the heavens and earth." At these times I have felt the Lord impress on me to return to the "old wells." To go back to those places where God so clearly spoke to me before.

I return to old prophecies that God has previously given. I listen to the things that previously stirred me, stirred my spirit, stirred my spirit to the point of demanding action. What does that look like for me? I listen to my old Keith Green vinyls. The originals from back in the early '80s when I first came to know Him, when I first felt called by God into the nations. I read some of my favourite Bible passages. I get out some of those old prophetic words spoken over me and refresh myself of the words He has already spoken over my life.

It is there, at those old wells, that I come before the presence of God once again. It is there that a fresh stirring takes place. Then I find the small flames of the fire in my belly are sparked and rise up once more. Once that fire is stoked, it is inevitable that the fire takes hold and God sends it wherever He wills. This fire is not for us to control. It is a wildfire—driven by the winds of His Holy Spirit.

In going back to Jesus calling his disciples to "follow Me, and I will make you fishers of men," we really need to ask ourselves, as Christians: if we are not fishing, are we really following?

God loves a missionary who says, "I haven't got a clue. I do not know; I don't know where to go, I don't know what to do, and I don't know what to say." It is at this point that God says, "Great, over to Me."

LOVE THY NEIGHBOUR

In following Jesus, to go wherever He leads doesn't always mean jumping on a plane and landing in a different nation. God may ask of us to be His face, just where we are. Earlier, I said my heart is still that of a missionary. Yet for the past fourteen years I have predominantly been living here in the UK, at my home. As well as taking time to work on myself, my function has been that of a social worker in child protection and now in mental health. I truly believe that is where God has caused me to be during this time in my life.

Although I am not allowed to overtly share the gospel with my clients, there is plenty of opportunity for me to walk in love and demonstrate His goodness. When people ask questions about spirituality, I respond. For the most part, it is just living the life.

My role as a social worker has taught me and stretched me by spending time with others, listening to their stories, doing my best for them to receive good outcomes, letting them know I see them. In general, all people want is to be truly seen and heard by you.

Jesus sat and listened to others. He reclined at the table and ate with them, spending time just being with others. No power encounters. More of being Himself in the everyday and allowing others to simply be themselves in His presence.

Loving can be a challenge, as I have found. Some people you naturally like and others you don't. There are times when you strongly dislike other people's behaviour. I am challenged to love unconditionally. God spoke to me about loving those who I think don't deserve it. When I sit and spend time with people who have behaved badly—abused their children, paedophiles, people who beat others badly, pimp their children out, deliberately starve their children, actively try to physically disable their children so they can get more money from the benefits agency, murderers, those who commit all sorts of crimes against others—I don't naturally warm to them. But, God spoke to me and said, "I love them just as much as I love you." God loves the oppressor as well as the oppressed. He loves the abuser as well as the abused. He loves the perp as well as the victim. I asked God to help me as I sit with them and respond to their needs with the same compassion as I do in other situations.

If you can say to yourself, "Today I followed Jesus and did all he asked of me," then you are in the right place; you are where He wants you to be.

THE HARVEST

"The harvest is plentiful and the workers are few. Therefore, beseech the Lord of the harvest to send out workers into the harvest field" (Matthew 9:37-38). People, it is time to go and bring in the harvest. Short term, long term, whatever—just go. They are waiting for you to show them Jesus. No ifs or buts. No hiding behind excuses, not even "spiritual" ones. Not even the one that says, "I'll pray for the harvest." It's great if you are an intercessor—but an intercessor "stands in the gap," so go and stand in the gap. Prayer is important but we must both pray and go. So, GO!

Therefore, in a nutshell, we are called to follow, commanded to go, and compelled by love.

The Rising

The Fisherman

CHAPTER NINE
IT'S BY NO MEANS THE END!

"Now to Him who is able to do super abundantly, far over and above all that we dare ask or think, infinitely beyond our highest prayers, desires, thoughts, hopes, and dreams . . ."

The Holy Bible

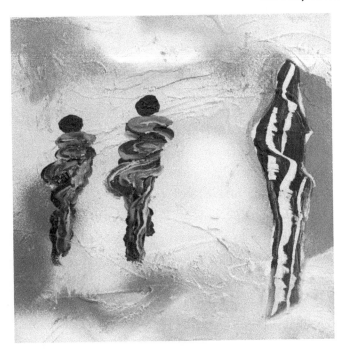

Travel On

IN THE SUMMER OF 2019 I had my fiftieth birthday. In the runup to it, at work, I attended two talks from drug company representatives. On both these occasions we were being informed about new drugs on the market for people with schizophrenia. Both representatives in their talk mentioned that people with schizophrenia are statistically more likely to die twenty years earlier than members of the general population. One even said, "So, for a person who is fifty years of age, it is the equivalent to that of being seventy." Other than my first thought which was "bloody charming," I also thought to myself, "I'm not having that." Hearing that spun me out. I was having a crisis. My response to this was to phone a personal trainer, and the following day, I started to exercise through the form of kickboxing. As it was a big birthday, my parents bought me, on my request, a stand up paddleboard (SUP), and I jumped on the water. I also made sure my fiftieth birthday itself was an active one. I went with family and close friends to the beach at Llangennith on Gower and spent the day bodyboarding in the surf, followed by a BBQ on the beach, of course!

HISTORY MAKERS

History has been shaped by people with mental health disorders just as much as those who have been perfectly sane. There have been the good, the gifted, and the despicable. I'll let you decide who falls into which category. Some say Joan of Arc was a schizophrenic. Others say Napoleon Bonaparte had a narcissistic personality disorder. Some have been "criminally insane" with psychopathic tendencies—Hitler, Himmler, Stalin, King Leopold II, Pol Pot, Vlad the Impaler and the cult leader, Jim Jones, to name a few. Vincent van Gogh suffered with bipolar/schizophrenia, and Beethoven and Isaac Newton experienced bipolar disorder. Winston Churchill and Abraham Lincoln suffered with depression. Charles Dickens had insomnia and depression, and he also had imaginary friends. Charles Darwin is said to have had a panic disorder with agoraphobia, depression, obsessive compulsive disorder ,and visual hallucinations. Sigmund Freud, neurologist, psychotherapist, and founder of psychoanalysis, had anxiety attacks and depression. He even heard his own name being called out to him. A number of celebrities of our times have spoken out about their mental health struggles, too. The Apostle Paul had a "thorn in his flesh," though whatever that was, we do not know; it could have been physical, emotional or mental. Although I have only named a few, it appears to me that some history makers that have been "afflicted," have just got on with it. I guess the trick is to make sure you are one of the good guys.

Up until now, I have told you my story without much comment or opinion. Now it is time for me to let loose, and I want to start with a warning!

A WARNING

Despite my good works which have driven me at times, I have also been concerned that my actions may cause some form of harm to others, although often I did not recognise it when others were swept up in my madness. My single-minded endeavours and pursuit to bring visions into reality have led me to focus on the goal, and in doing so, I lost sight not only of the needs of those close to me but also my own needs.

The following was taken from an assessment undertaken by mental health professionals during the diagnostic process:

"It could be that Laura invests almost every aspect of herself in her work, [her] beliefs and causes as a deflection away from the real problem, i.e., dealing with her own emotional needs . . . It could be that if Laura addresses her own emotional needs as opposed to dealing with others' needs all of her time, that she [will] come face to face with aspects of herself or her life that she finds uncomfortable, undesirable, or traumatic. . . . Based on the assessment, it is evident that Laura has dedicated her entire life to worthy causes and is clearly an individual who can offer others great comfort and sustenance in times of distress. Based on the difficulties Laura has experienced in her life, it is understandable that she has either not been able, or it has been too difficult for her, to attend to her own needs. This has subsequently manifested as mental ill health . . ."

Although this is not the cause of my mental health problems, the lack in attending to my own needs created an obstacle in my being able to deal with the issues I was experiencing.

For the last few years or so, I have taken a back seat, so to speak. I have not dashed here and there around the world on some mission or another. I have at times struggled to learn to be still, to remain in one place, and my work has been to attend to myself, to get to know myself, and to understand the nature of the beast that I have had to deal with. Yes, during this time, I have been working for Social Services , which in itself can be a highly demanding and stressful job. In doing so, I have been able to "minister" to others in a different way, under a different framework than I did in the twenty years prior to that. It is good to be presented with a warning, a warning that stops you in your tracks, causes you to think and act in a manner that addresses the issues at hand. For me, that was to come face to face with myself. Just me and me. In coming home to an empty house for the first time in my life, it has allowed me to be confronted with and deal with the person in the mirror with no interference from others, like those who have been well-meaning but unhelpful at times. When I have needed support, true friends have been there holding me up. Overwhelmingly, though, it has been something I have had to do for myself by myself. As you have seen for yourself, my failings are huge, and I continue to deal with issues of a faulty character and mental illness as they arise. But, I am dealing with them when I've been faced with them, rather than neglecting and overlooking them. If I had been of a different time, when life was shorter and risks of dying on the mission field were higher, a short life may not have required me to come face to face with and deal with myself. Given that we live in a time where life expectancy is longer, my better choice would be a more stable, well-balanced, rounded existence, free of distress and pain. Getting the foundations of one's life right is important for what is built on top. Safer not only for me, but also for those I come into contact with. For me, it has been important to invest time and energy on myself, to face my fears, and to deal with who I am, my illness, and the issues that are problematic and torment me.

EMBRACE CHANGE; IT'S A TIME FOR ACTION

Sometimes I wonder if what I see is great passion or great desperation. I ask myself, *Does it matter if it brings about change?* It is time to embrace change. It's time to step up, with vision, with purpose, to be targeted, to be planned, to rise, to have missions of purpose. We cannot judge the destination from the journey we are on. We are to be like a 4x4, designed to go off-road. Create a new road that others can travel down after you. Be a traveller, not a tourist, in this world.

Change is the cornerstone within the foundations of all social reform and social endeavours. Issues surrounding change, whether that change be natural or manufactured, are to be embraced in our personal walk and journey through life and also as we walk alongside others. Change can, along with other feelings, inspire hope. Hope, in turn, generates faith, enabling the desired action by an individual, a community, and even for a nation toward transformation.

When you Google the definition of change, a number of suggestions are highlighted. Here are a few. "To become different; take another instead of; get rid of; adopt new plan or option; take a new position." "Change" is very much an action word. *The Merriam-Webster Dictionary* also describes different forms of change; "putting on different clothing; passing to a different owner; to give or get money for an article." These forms of change, although ordinarily used in an entirely different context, are in fact totally relevant and hold symbolic significance. They speak of appearance, ownership, and cost.

Appearance: that which is seen by others. Replacing of one garment for another. Clothes can represent a time in life, an alliance with a particular group or culture, an outfit aiding a job or activity, even a hiding of that which is underneath. All symbolise possible needs to change.

Ownership raises questions of who or what is in control of your life or of our society. Are you taking responsibility for your own life? As a companion on the journey with others, are we giving tools and resources to empower and equip those we travel with? Are we taking ownership of our society and the general world around us, being responsible citizens?

Cost? Yes, it does! Change will always cost us something. What are you prepared to pay with?

Change is full of action and energy. Change creates. Change generates excitement and fear. Change is a process. Change is powerful. As a powerful source of creativity, change produces strong feelings and convictions within our own belief system. If change is to be embraced at any level, we must look at our past, the present, and the future. We must be willing to face the truth and find strength. We need to have an eager anticipation of the present moment.

We have no idea of what the future holds. We do not know how history will be shaped from tomorrow onwards. We can understand the past. Although it is often not good to dwell on the past, it does provide us with a picture of where we have been. It is today, in the present, when we decide enough is enough, and things can be better. I believe this, in turn, provides us with a snapshot of the future which is still being developed. At this time, we cannot clearly see the picture that is being processed; it is faint, it lacks colour, but it will continue to be developed, and it will become clear, contain vibrant colour. We hope, we believe, even with fear and trembling, that this snapshot of a possible future holds a picture that tells a story that defines us, that defines our generation for the good.

Programmes, training courses, rehabilitation centres, prison, psychiatric hospitals, spirituality, religions—these by themselves cannot change a person, however good they may be. Change only takes place from within a person, not from outside. The person seeking change must first desire it, and yet a want can be weak and waver at the slightest opposition. Desire can find itself lacking. It is as though a light needs to be switched on. When this happens, we are enlightened. In the light, we receive revelations, and the penny of realisation drops. We have a conviction that 1) things need not necessarily be the way they are right now and 2) one day things will be better. Both passionate and desperate desire are all-consuming. Passion and desperation provide an energy to climb mountains and swim shark-infested seas to reach what is desired. It can be argued that passion generates positive energy and desperation generates negative energy, but I am not sure that is always the case. Self-awareness—an intuitive sense of where we are, how far we have progressed—brings about confidence and maturity. Awareness and opportunities open the door to the ability to choose. By choice, not by chance, we move towards the fulfilment of our destiny.

The truth is, we are in control, and we have choices to make. We make choices even when we tell ourselves we cannot choose, we cannot decide. Be it consciously or unconsciously, we make choices. In deciding or in feeling unable to make a choice, is actually a choice in itself. Some of us can sabotage anything and everything that is good in our lives, because we are our own worst enemy. It's upsetting when you realise this, it's difficult when you see that you have caused yourself pain and have taken away your own joy. Let us focus on the positive in this situation: if we can cause ourselves misery, then we must be able to generate and create new and fresh joy, happiness, peace in our lives. I believe this to be true; we have choices to make.

I have asked myself questions, seeking answers. In my search for answers, I have often found the unexpected, and it appears that I need to be satisfied that not all questions have answers. It is important to understand that, when you suffer with a severe and enduring mental illness, you do not choose for depression, mania, and hallucinations to take over your life. You are not to blame, it is not your fault, you have not done something wrong, you have not brought it upon yourself. I think it is foolishness to say about these severe illnesses, "I control them," because in reality, "they often control me." We do not choose to be afflicted in such a way. That would be like saying, "I choose to have cancer." No one would choose that. Mental illness is a cancer. It is a cancer of the mind and the soul. There are mental illnesses from which some recover fully, and there are mental illnesses that remain with a person to differing degrees throughout their lives. I believe it is our response to these crippling, debilitating, flooring illnesses where we can find choice playing a part and having a role. I am certainly not saying it is easy. There can be multiple factors involved in coming to a decision, making a choice, and seeing change take place. It takes much soul-searching and heartache.

We need to create an environment for change to take place. Whether you admit it to yourself or not, we all have a need to be loved, accepted, and valued. These are fundamental needs of all of mankind, from paupers to princes, you will find this to be so. We are all unique; no two of us are the same. Differences can clearly be seen. In creating an environment for change, we need to be non-judgmental, accepting of others as they are. There is no place for prejudice. Respect for the beliefs, views, opinions, styles, cultures, backgrounds, and choices of others is hugely important. It is about being selfless and empathic.

Change is experienced in many forms. Change can be constant and ongoing, change can take time. Change can also be sudden and radical. Influences that bring about change in the life of an individual, a community, or a nation are equally varied. History has produced many men and women who have been social reformers and revolutionists. They have been people with a vision of hope that things can be better, people who have dramatically changed the world by their passion and personal sacrifices, people who struggled with choices and convictions of the heart, and people stirred to action, their beliefs inspiring others by hope, faith, and love.

The question to be considered is, where will your hope, passion, and choices take you? Ask yourself—when was the last time you did something for the first time? And remember, it's dead fish that go with the flow.

THE DIAGNOSIS—WHAT I REALLY THINK

As we have already established, medics have given me a diagnosis of schizoaffective disorder. I am afflicted with symptoms of schizophrenia and bipolar disorder. I am in agreement that I am a voice hearer, and I see visions. I also experience highs and lows in my moods. I have faced death on more than one occasion. I am told that what I hear and see is not real. I am asked if I know that, if I understand that? As I have said to my own psychiatrist, "being a mental health professional, Monday to Friday, 9 to 5, of course, it's not real, that's what the medical model says."

It was 2012 when I was given this diagnosis. But 2012 was not when the symptoms associated with this illness started. When I look back over my life, it started in my teen years and continued with me throughout my life and continues to be the case today. The diagnosis of 2012 was when everything finally started to make sense.

However, I do not fully subscribe to the understanding that a medical model provides. Psychiatry, by using medication, as well as other forms of treatment, seeks to bring a person back to "normality." But what is normality? I do wonder if I am being manipulated into being someone who would be considered "acceptable" by the masses. Who are they to decide what is normal? Why should I conform? Who says my thinking, actions, and behaviour are "off the wall" and "mad"?

Nevertheless, I can see at times that my mental state becomes too much to bear and I have even lost my mental capacity. In the first instance, acceptance that I have this mental illness was an obstacle I had to overcome. It was a difficult process, it was a place of surrender—everything that I once believed was stripped away. Due to my own negative images, false beliefs, and lack of understanding, I struggled. Nevertheless, I felt there was more to the paradigm which was being provided by the doctors.

What medics call my mental illness, I see as my superpower; I can hear and see things that other people cannot. I have times of amazing energy and high productivity. Someone once said to me, "If I can only get to work with 5 percent of you, it's like 95 percent of some others." When I suffer with what we call depression, I experience a personal closeness and intimacy with God. My so-called low times are actually high times, spiritually speaking, when I feel the presence of a greater being. I see it as a gift, one which many others do not have. I do not believe all of my experiences are due to illness. I see some as "spiritual" and some are "just me." I see some of my so-called concerning and bizarre behaviours as symbolic in nature. Language and communication are more than words. Actions, groans, drums, all speak and have a language of their own. In Africa they have the "jungle drums" that send out a message to all those who hear them. Here in the West, we have a well-known saying: "Actions speak louder than words." So why is it then, when someone speaks through actions, that people freak out? The snakes and the scorpions don't talk to me in English or any other language, not even snake language. That would be mad! They are there and they may occasionally attack. So, is it not logical to try and protect yourself from them? I hear you say, "But, they are not real." I say, "Oh, really? They are very much real to me." It's a bit like this: when Blaze and I went to Japan, we went up Mount Fuji. In the souvenir shop, we bought a "can of air from Mount Fuji." Some would say, "That's a joke. It's an empty can with absolutely nothing in it." Others would say, "It is was it says on the tin, a can of air. We better not open it when we get back to Wales, because we would lose the Mount Fuji air, and it would be mixed in with and may disappear in the Welsh air, then we would have a can of Mount Snowji or Mount Fudon"! If you can't see it, if you can't hear it, if you can't touch it, if you can't taste it, if you can't smell it, does it mean it is not there?

I can see the snakes and scorpions, as well as my other sightings. It is my reality; it may not be yours, but it is mine. Maybe from a position of faith, I have an insight, a prophetic edge? I was flicking through the channels on the TV one day and came across *Songs of Praise*. The presenter was interviewing a vicar on the topic of prophets. The presenter asked, "Where are the prophets today?" The vicar replied, "You will find some of them in psychiatric hospitals with a diagnosis of schizophrenia." That pricked my ears up and made me think. I do accept that there is, however, an element of illness, and I continue to take my medication as prescribed, like a good girl. Although I choose to take my medication, it does not entirely sit right with me. I simply do not see illness as the only dynamic at play. Maybe in saying this, it proves the medic's right. I'm just "bonkers"!?!

I choose to focus on positives, not negatives. I acknowledge the negatives—the torment, the despair, the harm, the near-death experiences. They cause distress not only to me but to others around me. But look at the positives; there are many, and I choose to focus on them. I refuse to be defined by my diagnosis. I will not allow it to limit me.

People have always referred to me as being eccentric, quirky, and different. It has been said, even in the midst of people who are considered "different," that I am the odd one out. Is that due to my so-called mental illness? No, I don't think so—that's just the way I am. Personally, I don't identify with being either eccentric or quirky, I can't see it at all.

I am learning to live with me, accepting myself as I am. I once looked for a miracle in the form of an extraordinary event, a supernatural phenomenon taking away and removing that which I found to be undesirable. I didn't see the real miracle of the amazing and wonderful occurrence in loving myself in full knowledge and recognition of the good, bad, and ugly within my own soul—that of my mind, my will, and my emotions. Where I once saw weakness that I wanted to reject, I now see strength.

DISCRIMINATION, OPPRESSION, AND EMPOWERMENT

The world wants to give us labels, but the world also discriminates against us based on these labels. For some, a diagnosis is helpful; for others, it is not. Discrimination treats individuals or groups in a way that is worse than the way people are usually treated. It is unfair and unequal treatment of others that renders people powerless. In doing so, cracks and divisions appear in our society. Discrimination is more than just prejudice and inequalities, because power that allows injustice also plays a part. Mental illness, disability, gender, age, class, race, religion—we are diverse, and diversity is something that should be celebrated.

However, we often find that our differences become a source of oppression. Oppression can be unjust and cruel. It is degrading, demeaning, negative, and inhuman. Oppression is a power play that seeks to keep those subject to it low. It affects individual lives and society as a whole; it attacks one's identity. It seeks to marginalise, isolate, exclude, and alienate, destroying confidence and self-esteem. It can have an impact on life-chances, job prospects, economic position and social standing. Oppression is complex with a host of factors in play.

Stereotypes fuelled by reports and images in the media do not help. Schizophrenics particularly get a raw deal, branded in front page headlines and in the movies as highly dangerous, mad axe murderers. As well as spinning a lie and false information, stereotypes generate fear in the general public's eye. Yes, we have to weigh the risk associated with psychotic illnesses, but most people with the diagnostic label of schizophrenia are not a danger in such dramatic fashion.

The medical model and psychiatric service can in themselves be oppressive, dispassionate, dismissive, and can even be discriminatory in practice. I think my own experience as a patient on an acute psychiatric ward highlights that can be the case. I am not saying all psychiatric services and all mental health professionals operate in such a manner. I was directly supported under mental health services for five years, being treated in the community for the most part. I had my own Community Psychiatric Nurse (CPN) who saw me for either weekly, fortnightly, or monthly appointments, depending on the needs of my mental health at that time. I had one CPN who, over a period of a year, only actually turned up for 50 percent of her own appointments with me. I had another CPN who would threaten me, at regular intervals, with hospital admission, and if I refused to go, she would have me "sectioned." She was also very pushy in trying to get me to have a depot injection rather than taking oral medication. Maybe that was an indication of where my mental health and compliance to treatment was at the time, but I found her confrontational manner to be less than helpful. On the depot issue, I refused again and again as I felt that if I were to receive the injection it would take control away from me. That was my personal opinion at that time. I have to say that now I see things from a different angle and perspective; the depot injection is actually an effective method of treatment and less hassle for the patient insofar as you don't need to remember to take your medicine on a daily basis, and when you are refusing to do so the medicine is already in you, thus helping the patient to get or keep well. I also had a CPN who appeared totally disinterested in me and only saw me for five minutes once a month. I really didn't see the point in that. Some have come into my home with an all-knowing, all-wise, "I am the professional," arrogant, self-important attitude. With regards to my experience of being a patient under the Crisis Team, to be brutally honest, I thought, *what a waste of space they were.* Considering I was only under their service because I was "in crisis," they were less than proactive. They phone and, if you don't pick up or miss the call, then that's it, nothing, not another call, no visit. When they do visit, they come just too quickly, check you have taken your medication, and then go. They did not stop to chat and really find out how I was doing. When you phone them, there is no one there to answer your call. Having said all that, there are very good doctors, nurses, CPNs, Approved Mental Health Professionals (AMHPs), and social workers, among other roles performed within mental health services in the hospitals, in the Community Mental Health Teams and the Crisis Team as well as the Emergency Duty Team. I have also come across wonderful individuals who work in support and voluntary services with people with mental health conditions. Many do adopt an anti-discriminatory approach and seek to empower their patients and clients in the work they undertake with them. Nevertheless, this style of practice is not always the experience that patients receive. In working in a Community Mental Health Team in secondary services that work with people with severe and enduring mental illnesses, my colleagues are a great bunch of individuals. I have learnt many a valuable lesson and witnessed some extremely good practice that has aided and challenged my own practice. However, there have been things I have heard in the office that would make you wince, and there have been occasions where I felt strongly enough to challenge a colleague or two on what they had just said in their blind sweeping statements. Of course, there are some things that go with the black sense of humour that you will find in most professions that deal with people. I certainly don't take myself too seriously and will be one of the first to have a joke at my own expense. But even in that humour, it can promote an atmosphere of discrimination and oppression.

We need to establish a base of equality and social justice. We are required to bridge the gap with a sound knowledge base, develop solid attitudes and values, and stimulate open and honest dialogue. Discrimination and oppression will seek to silence us, but we must not be silenced. It is time to stand in the gap, address the power imbalance, make your own voice heard, and be a voice that advocates for the oppressed. In doing so, it will reframe the cultural, social, systematic, structural, and political landscape. It is time to be empowered and see a radically different alternative.

SHAME

Discrimination is a form of oppression; it comes upon us from the outside. Shame is a form of oppression within us. Shame is a stain that does not wash out. A thousand showers cannot wash away that stain. Shame is an attack against yourself, against your core inner being. It attacks the "I am's" and the "I can's." Shame says, "I am worthless. There is nothing that I can do that is of any worth or value. I am useless." If you find yourself thinking these things or when walking alongside someone who not only says these things about themselves but truly believes it, ask yourself: are you encountering an enemy called shame that seeks to slay?

Shame hinders and stops us moving forward. In searching for the meaning of shame, many definitions can be found. Here is a selection I have put together. Shame *is a deep, painful mental feeling of a sense of doing something either improper, dishonourable, or ridiculous; it is a feeling of humiliation and distress, feelings that are a mix of regret, self-hate and dishonour. Shame encompasses the entire self.* We must not confuse shame with guilt. Shame is an attack on who you are whereas guilt is an attack on what you have done.

Shame causes an emotional distance or separation from 1) a facet of oneself and 2) one's experience.

Shame causes you to supress and deny. In shame, you have to face the truth, and ultimately, you will be free. Our conscience needs to be re-awakened. Shame cuts off spontaneity, joy, life, energy, excitement, trust, belief, and freedom. Shame causes us to look at ourselves as unimportant, inadequate, not good enough.

We are required to come to a place where we have a complete turnaround and thus go in the opposite direction. But how do we achieve this?

In December 2002, I helped Santa out and went to work for the Royal Mail sorting the Christmas post. Word got around that I was the chaplain for Asda, the supermarket. I was surprised by the number of people who came alongside me and told me their life stories. In one week, three people wanted to know if they could be forgiven—one even asked if I could forgive them. Although I was surprised and amazed by this, many people need to realise the power there is in forgiveness. There is forgiveness that can be bestowed by others, and there is forgiveness we can give to ourselves. For some of us, our conscience torments us. We can be exonerated from all blame in the eyes of others and even the law, but we cannot find peace. We cannot forgive ourselves. If we want to move forward, we need to let ourselves off the hook, stop beating ourselves up, and let go. Forgiveness holds deep significance. There are times when we are required to forgive others, there are occasions when we ask others to forgive us, and there are times when we must forgive ourselves. Grief, pain, and sorrow can be washed away with an act of kindness, an act of forgiveness. Forgiveness wipes away the nightmare, the terrors found in darkness. Forgiveness does not forget, condone, or excuse. Forgiveness is powerful. The hardest form of forgiveness is often self-forgiveness.

Shame and forgiveness go hand in hand. In identifying and presenting you with a problem, I have offered a solution. As shame is more than simple embarrassment, forgiveness is more than simply putting something in the past. Forgiveness is for our own growth and happiness. Self-forgiveness frees us from the inner regret, anger, and hatred.

How do we forgive ourselves? For me, it was about coming to a place where I learnt to love myself. For me as a Christian, it was about understanding God's love for me and to see His father's heart towards me. Jesus preached on two commandments: 1) to love God and 2) to love your neighbour as you love yourself. It therefore goes without saying: how can you truly love your neighbour if you do not love yourself? If you want to move into an effective ministry and serve others, you first need to learn to love yourself.

LOSS AND NEW LIFE

Mental illness, if untreated, can leave a trail of destruction. In the wake of that destruction, we can lose things and people who are very dear to us. It can wreak havoc in every area of our lives, the most important being the impact on our relationships. I have lost people I once called friends. I have a lost marriage. I lost years in the life of my daughter. I have also lost my vocation within the church ministry. Since my hospital admissions, I have not undertaken any further overseas missions, and I have not stood in the pulpit and preached. Out of these losses, though, the greatest and most significant loss—my relationship with my daughter—has been restored. That, far beyond everything else, is what I care about the most.

Mental illness is unpredictable in nature. Although I may be well today, there are no guarantees that that will remain the case. I continue to do all the right things, but in a blink of an eye, regardless of my efforts, that may change. I have a backup plan should my mental health deteriorate significantly. My thought process is, *If I lose my job because I am so unwell, I will have no money; if I have no money, I can't pay my mortgage; if I can't pay my mortgage, I lose my house; if I lose my house, I have my van. If you ever see an orange VW T25 pulled off the road, honk your horn as you go past—it might be me!*

These days, I have no desire to run. I have come to the realisation that you can run but you can't hide from yourself. I used to have a "go-bag," because I thought other people would be better off without me. I had a plan, so if I felt it necessary, I would disappear. I did not know where I would go, but I knew not to take anything with me whereby I could be traced and found—no bank cards, no mobile cell phone, no car. When I was a child, I hid camping equipment under my bed. I had a book of camping craft that instructed me on how to make a shelter, how to catch and cook food, how to make furniture from sticks. I decided that should I run away, the woods would be the place to go.

I had felt, at one time, that even my daughter would be better off without me. One night, I went into her room as she slept. I stood over her cot. I told her how sorry I was for being a useless mother who would only let her down again and again. I told her I loved her and said goodbye. The voices were saying, *She doesn't need you, you are a useless mother, you will cause her nothing but pain, take yourself from her, she is better off without you, go, go do it, now is the time, go do it, it's easy, just take a few pills.* I went into my room and took an overdose. My tears and despair caused me to cough and choke. I threw up the pills. I later went back into my baby's bedroom. I picked her up. She remained asleep. I told her how much I loved her and that I would never leave her.

I have made a new life for myself as I have a more stable and balanced approach. I make time to do things that I enjoy for myself. Although I never saw myself owning a house, I have made a home that I like, and I enjoy my garden. I have new friendships as well as maintaining some of the old. I surround myself with people who are good for me. I have people who encourage me. There are people who appear to enjoy my company, sitting and chatting around the fire, people who relate to me for who I am, not because of what I do. I have people I go camping with and I have people who enjoy water sports with me. I have some who keep me in check and help to ground me, but I don't associate myself with dream stealers.

Over time, people come and go, but in true friendship, a mark of joy is left deep within your soul, in your heart. Having the right people around you to encourage, support, and laugh with is immensely important in helping you to rise up and soar on wings as the eagle. Friendship lifts you to new heights and overlooks your broken parts. It sees and admires the flowers in your garden rather than focusing on the weeds. Hope, strength, and courage stir and enable us to conquer fear and overcome pain and despair that seeks to swallow us up.

I still dream and wonder what life has for me. I believe there are dreams that die; they go under the ground and cannot be seen on the surface. With new growth, they become bigger and better than they were before. I had a small palm tree planted by my pond in the garden. A *Cordyline Australis* Red Star, I believe. It died and disappeared. I was disappointed but just thought to myself, *Sometimes plants don't take, it's a tropical plant, and I live in wet Wales, say no more!* For some time, nothing was seen above surface, and then one spring, to my surprise, it started to grow again. It is now a tree. I didn't plant a tree in the first place—just a small little palm that died. I had no idea what was happening under the ground, no idea of what the plant would grow into. Sometimes the voices speak a certain level of wisdom, have good ideas, and are encouraging. I heard a voice saying, "The dreams, the vision, was too small and had to go through a death process. What is going to come out is better than what went into the ground."

In my life, my parents have been a source of inspiration to me. During their mid-to-late seventies, they have been going on mission trips to the Ukraine. They have been part of a team that has been building a children's home. They both have been engaging in practical work as well as interacting with host families and churches, bringing encouragement and hope. My old mother has been extremely active mixing plaster, getting it ready for the guys to skim the walls, which at her age is quite something. I have found personal encouragement and hope and I am inspired by their example insofar as realising age is no barrier. You are never too old as you are never too young. I reckon that on this basis I could have another thirty years of service in having missions of purpose. This excites me.

DISCOVERING NEW DIMENSIONS

Those who have gone before us have provided us with models of understanding to help us navigate a way through the choppy seas of mental illness into the calm of a place called "recovery."

There are two largely used models that shape services in the field of mental health. The medical model is the dominant model. It is a biomedical or disease model. Treatment provided in the form of medication and talking therapies is the most common form of intervention. Then there is the social/psychosocial model. Perspectives look at the interaction between social disadvantage and mental disorder, and labelling, amongst others as explanations. This model looks at the social and environmental causes. It is suggested that a combination of these models is the most effective way ahead rather than one route or the other. Within these models we have been provided with legislation in a bid to protect us from our own vulnerability and to safeguard our human rights. Getting to know what they are can be helpful. I look back on my own detention in a psychiatric hospital in 2011. Officially, I was there as a voluntary/informal patient. I would argue whether indeed it was really voluntary, because I was threatened with being "sectioned" if I tried to leave. I also question whether I had the mental capacity, in the first instance, in being able to make an informed decision about going into hospital. Certainly this was true the first time, as I cannot even remember how I got there. This leads me to question whether I was able to make a judgement on my own condition. On another occasion, when I left A&E and returned home, the police were called to find me and bring me back to hospital so I could be admitted on the psychiatric ward. Leaving hospital and refusing to go with the police does not sound like volunteering to go into hospital. Yet again, threats were used in getting me there.

A third model is a psycho-spiritual approach. This is not really tapped into in secondary services. If you are in a position where you are provided with a Care and Treatment Plan, there is opportunity for your religious and spiritual beliefs and needs to feature in that plan. One of the sections contained within this document is titled "Social, Cultural, Spiritual." This opens the door not only to express your beliefs, but also to state how these beliefs work to comfort and help you in times of crisis. If you find that in times of mental turmoil you need to pray, then your plan should say so. I have seen this situation arise. To observe and witness a "non-believer" telling a person of faith to go and pray because that is what their care plan says they need to do, is, well, quite incredible—it makes me smile. But should it be incredible? Why is it not an accepted "normal" approach?

I feel it is a shame this model is not fully embraced, and although it is a dimension that has been identified, it remains a dimension that is lost at this time. I wonder if a lack of the practitioner's confidence that produces a feeling of not being the expert hinders this approach in moving forward. The pretty much non-existent training in this area for professionals working in the field does not help either.

The Royal College of Psychiatrists state that they are "becoming increasingly aware of ways in which some aspects of spirituality can offer real benefits for mental health." They continue by advising the professional that "A spiritual assessment should be considered as part of every mental health assessment . . .Mental health professionals also need to be able to distinguish between a spiritual crisis and a mental illness, particularly when these overlap . . . exploring spiritual issues can be therapeutic in itself." Suggestions of opening questions by the professional to the patient have been offered in setting the scene, in looking at the past, the present, the future, and in determining the next steps.

Whatever role you play in the care of people with mental health conditions, I would encourage you to step up, be brave, and embrace the spiritual dynamic in the lives of those you seek to serve. You do not even need to be a spiritual person yourself, but you can acknowledge, recognise, and give value to this aspect of people's lives that is so core and central. In doing so, you will find change, recovery, and even healing.

For those of us who suffer, we are the experts on our own mental health problems. We may not know the answers, but we do know and experience the effects of the symptoms. When we are both spiritual and have a mental health condition, it can be hard at times to distinguish between the two, in all honesty. Spiritual encounters and psychosis can be areas where we find ourselves questioning what is going on. It can also be difficult for those around us as to whether they should be concerned for us or not. It is not only difficult at times for our loved ones, but also for professionals as they seek to help and assist. There needs to be a growing ability to discern and a knowledge base to be able to act upon. It is important that we do not lose a sense of reality. It is okay to have your head in the heavens, so to speak, as long as your feet are firmly on the ground. In being grounded, we need to be anchored. It is for us as individuals to identify the things that anchor us. That may be different for each of us as individuals. But we all do need to be grounded. If we lose our sense of reality, we can descend into madness.

There is a lot we do not know about mental ill health. There is a lot professionals do not know about mental disorders. A paradigm shift is required. I can't help but think there is so much more for us to learn and discover.

When it comes to seeing visions and hearing voices, as with what someone may physically feel, taste, or smell that others do not, I do find myself asking the question, *Where is the line between the phenomenon driven by psychosis and the encounters found with spirituality?*

Our perspectives hold importance. When you see an old person, let's say a ninety-year-old, what do you see? Do you say, "Ah, bless" or "Oh, wow"? Do you have pity on the "dear old lady," or do you want to sit at her feet and learn of the wisdom she has to give? Perspectives on what we already have access to are important, but I believe we need to open our minds to new perspectives, new understandings, new ways of working.

My mentor, my friend, Christine, is sadly in care with dementia. Her husband John posts videos of his visits with her on his Facebook page. Christine has diminished mental cognition, her speech is impaired, and her physical abilities are limited. Every visit, John, along with one of their daughters, spends time singing spiritual hymns with Christine. Given the extent of her dementia, what occurs is truly remarkable. Christine tries and does sing along: "Amazing grace how sweet the sound . . ." So, what is happening? Christine's spirit is very much alive and active. As they sing, Christine's spirit connects with the spirit of God. They experience a shared spiritual encounter in the love of their Lord Jesus. She is truly a spiritual giant!

In severe mental illnesses, I believe the spirit of a person which is alive to God cannot be taken. Be it in Christine's case or my own, when much has been robbed from us—even when we have lost our mental capacity—

the illness cannot rob us of our spirit. That is ours, it belongs to a higher being, it is alive and active. When we are in the darkest of days, we are able to connect spirit to spirit.

For those of you who are carers or observers looking in from the outside, no doubt there are times when you are overcome with immense sadness, hopelessness, and despair. Your own soul may be in turmoil and be downcast. In the depths of my illness, I may be silent, and when I do speak, it may be total gibberish and you are unable to understand a word I say. I would encourage you to look beyond seeing me as a physical being, and rather see me as a spiritual being. If you are able to do that in the face of adversity, you will find hope and peace. At the end of the day, it is my firm belief that our spirit is the most important thing. Our spirit is the source of life itself. Do not worry for my spirit. My spirit is in the hands of my heavenly father. It is a place of love and safety. He will not let me go.

As you have read through my story, it is clear that there is a spiritual perspective to my life. All of us are able to connect to the spiritual realm. Our spirituality can help us find meaning and purpose. It can also bring hope and healing at times of suffering. For me, the connection I have with Jesus and the relationship I have with God is what has made the difference. It is in this relationship that I feel safe and secure. I feel valued and loved. You, too, can experience this love and acceptance. You, too, can have a God-given plan and purpose for your life.

HOPE, COURAGE, FAITH

Hope generates faith. Hope believes that one day things will be better. There may be times when you have heard yourself say, "I hope so." This statement is some form of a question. We are uncertain what the actual answer is. We hope for the best but fear for the worst. Hope is not sure. Faith knows that one day things will be better. Faith is solid. In the darkest of storms, faith breaks through. Faith is being able to face the facts without being put off by them. Unless you come face to face with reality and truth, you can't move into a place of faith. Reality can be crushing, but mixed with a dose of faith, it can lead us to a place of security, openness, and trust.

We all fall down from time to time, and I know when I do, it can be quite spectacular. However, it is not the falling down; it is the getting up that counts. The greater the struggle, the greater the breakthrough, the greater the victory. The darker it is, the more powerful the light that shines through. In the hours of darkness, we can be sure of that light that pierces the black space around us. If you switch on a torch in the midday sun it is difficult to see that light on at all. It has little effect. But put on that some torch in the middle of the night, and the power of that source of light illuminates your path and guides your every step.

Do not lose heart. Do not lose your courage when you come face to face with your imperfections. Have the courage to face the truth, the courage to change the things that should be changed. Be fearless. Live life fearlessly. Keep pressing on beyond your fear. Fear is a liar. Triumph over fear. Have the fearless spirit of a conqueror.

Faith creates an environment where healing can take place. Faith is not about what circumstances or feelings say. Replace the spirit of fear with the spirit of joy. Joy is not an emotion—it is a state of being. Build a healthy, strong self-image. Know you are valued, loved, accepted, and gifted. If you have a negative self-image, faith will be found lacking. Confess who you are. Speak it out loud. Faith speaks and has a language of its own. By faith, a new thing will occur within us and through us.

GIVING

Fan into flame the gifts within you. The fire within is our drive, the passion in our veins, the spring in our step. We all have good qualities within us, things we are good at, characteristics that make us a good person. From one person to another, those gifts differ. We were not designed to be islands. However independent and self-sufficient we are, we need one another.

Consider yourself as a pool of water. A body of water may have an inlet pipe. This inlet pipe is like that which we receive. So the outlet pipe is that which we give out. A pool of water needs an outlet or it becomes stagnant. Water is a critical element that causes things to grow and brings life. Without water, things shrivel up and die. No living thing can survive without water. Water purity is crucial, and it is aided with the ebb and flow. As water flows in, it must also flow out. Therefore, as you receive, so you also give.

Be an encourager. Be the inspiration for others to fight on. When others are facing defeat and thinking about giving up, come alongside and fire them up. By coming alongside at this critical time, breakthrough and victory will take place. It's a strategy of war. When an army was flagging in battle, a person whose role it was to encourage the troops and stir them up to go back into battle would come alongside. This is identified in the Greek word *parakletos*—*para* meaning alongside, and *kletos*, to call, thus giving us the meaning of "to call alongside." This is a word used in the Bible for the word "counsellor." The "encourager" is one of four definitions for this word *parakletos*. It was actually used in describing the nature of the Holy Spirit. It is my belief that it is also a challenge for us, whoever we are, whatever we believe—a challenge for all mankind, an edification to inspire us to adopt the heart of an encourager, to be a person that builds up, not tears down.

What is your plan of action—your personal mission statement? Don't stink like a stagnant pond. Let the water of life from within you flow.

WILDFIRE

"It's okay if you fall down and you lose your spark. Just make sure that when you get back up you rise as the whole damn fire."
Unknown

I heard a voice keep repeating the word wildfire, "Wildfire, wildfire, wildfire." I asked him, "What do you mean?" There was no reply. I hate it when they don't answer back on something that could be important to know. In the silence, I was left to my own thoughts. I pondered on the word wildfire. I was led to this conclusion:

Wildfire is uncontrollable, strong. and spreads quickly. When ignited, it is difficult to extinguish. It allows important nutrients to return to the soil, enabling new healthy beginnings in which life flourishes. Yes, wildfire is destructive, but let the damage burn up the debris caused by the havoc that lays to waste on the ground of lives robbed by what is called mental illness. Historically, wildfires started by humans were used in warfare.

Be stirred. Let us ignite a flame that develops into a wildfire spreading across our lives, our community, and the nation, bringing about shoots of new life. Let us raise a shout of a warrior. Courage found in the heart of a warrior is contagious. My warrior cry:

"There ain't no grave gonna hold my body down!"
—*Bethel Music*

INFORMATION ON:
SCHIZOAFFECTIVE DISORDER

WITH PERMISSION, THE FOLLOWING HAS been taken from the *Rethink* factsheet. Information on mental health disorders and so much more can be found on their website.

www.rethink.org

Rethink Mental Illness.

factsheet

SCHIZOAFFECTIVE DISORDER

Schizoaffective disorder is a mental illness that affects your moods and thoughts. This factsheet explains the condition, possible causes, and treatments. This factsheet is for people with schizoaffective disorder. And for their carers, relatives, and friends.

Key
Points.

- Schizoaffective disorder has symptoms of schizophrenia and bipolar disorder.
- Your symptoms can be psychosis with mania and depression.
- No one knows what causes schizoaffective disorder. Research shows that genetic and environmental factors can increase your risk of getting a mental illness.
- There are different types of schizoaffective disorder.
- Your mental health team should offer you medication and talking therapies.
- Your mental health team should help you to learn how to manage your symptoms.

1. WHAT IS SCHIZOAFFECTIVE DISORDER?

Schizoaffective disorder is a mental illness that can affect your thoughts, mood, and behaviour. You may have symptoms of bipolar disorder and schizophrenia. These symptoms may be mania, depression, and psychosis.

About one in 200 people develop schizoaffective disorder at some time during their life. It tends to develop during early adulthood. And it is more common in women than men.

You can find out more information about:

- Psychosis
- Bipolar disorder
- Schizophrenia
- Depression

at www.rethink.org. Or call our General Enquiries Team on 0121 522 7007 and ask them to send you a copy of our factsheet.

2. HOW IS SCHIZOAFFECTIVE DISORDER DIAGNOSED?

A psychiatrist will diagnose schizoaffective disorder through a mental health assessment. You may get a diagnosis for schizoaffective disorder if you have depressive or manic symptoms with schizophrenic symptoms.

Psychiatrists will use the following manuals to help to diagnose you:

- International Classification of Diseases (ICD-10) produced by the World Health Organisation (WHO)
- Diagnostic and Statistical Manual (DSM-5) produced by the American Psychiatric Association

The manuals are guides which explain different mental health conditions. They also explain symptoms of the conditions and how long certain symptoms should last before a diagnosis should be made.

You may have had a combination of both psychotic symptoms with bipolar symptoms to get a schizoaffective disorder diagnosis. However, your symptoms should be clearly present for at least two weeks.

3. WHAT ARE THE SYMPTOMS OF SCHIZOAFFECTIVE DISORDER?

Symptoms of schizoaffective disorder are:

MANIC SYMPTOMS

You may experience the following if you have mania:

- Feeling happy or positive, even if things are not going well for you
- Feeling overly active, energetic or restless
- Feeling more irritable than usual
- Feeling much better about yourself than usual
- Talking very quickly, jumping from one idea to another or having racing thoughts

- Being easily distracted and struggling to focus on one topic
- Not needing much sleep
- Thinking you can do much more than you actually can
- Doing things you normally wouldn't which can cause problems, such as spending lots of money, having casual sex with different partners, using drugs or alcohol, gambling or making unwise business decisions
- Being much more social than usual
- Being argumentative, pushy, or aggressive

DEPRESSIVE SYMPTOMS

You may feel the following if you have depression:

- Low mood
- Less energy, tired, or "slowed down"
- Hopeless or negative feelings
- Guilty, worthless, or helpless feelings
- Less interest in things you normally like to do
- Difficulty concentrating, remembering, or making decisions
- Restlessness or irritability
- Sleeping too much, not being able to sleep or having disturbed sleep
- Being more or less hungry than usual, or have a weight change
- Thinking of death or suicide, or attempting suicide

SCHIZOPHRENIC SYMPTOMS

Schizophrenia is a mental illness which affects the way you think. Symptoms can have an effect on how to cope with day-to-day life. Symptoms include:

- **Hallucinations.** You may hear, see, or feel things that are not there.
- **Delusions.** You may believe things that are not true.
- **Disorganised speech.** You may begin to talk quickly or slowly,

and the things you say might not make sense to other people. You may switch topics without any obvious link.

- **Disorganised behaviour.** You may wear clothes that are not appropriate to the weather. You may act inappropriately to other people, such as laugh if they tell you sad news.
- **Catatonic behaviour.** You may feel unable to move or appear to be in daze.
- **Negative symptoms.** You may find it hard to think straight.

You can find out more information about:

- Psychosis
- Bipolar disorder
- Schizophrenia
- Depression

at www.rethink.org. Or call our General Enquiries Team on 0121 522 7007 and ask them to send you a copy of our factsheet.

4. ARE THERE DIFFERENT TYPES OF SCHIZOAFFECTIVE DISORDER?

There are three main types of schizoaffective disorder:

Manic type—A schizoaffective disorder manic type diagnosis means you have symptoms of schizophrenia and mania at the same time through a period of illness.

Depressive type—A schizoaffective disorder depressive type means you have symptoms of schizophrenia and depression at the same time through a period of illness.

Mixed type—A diagnosis of schizoaffective disorder mixed type means you have symptoms of schizophrenia, depression, and mania when you are unwell.

5. WHAT CAUSES SCHIZOAFFECTIVE DISORDER?

Psychiatrists do not know what causes schizoaffective disorder. But we do know that you will have a chemical imbalance in your brain if you have the condition. Research shows that genetic and environmental factors can increase your risk of developing the illness.

GENETIC FACTORS

Schizoaffective disorder is slightly more common if other members of your family have schizophrenia, schizoaffective disorder, or bipolar disorder. This suggests that genetics may have a role to play in the development of schizoaffective disorder.

ENVIRONMENTAL FACTORS

Environmental factors are things that happen to an individual in life. It is thought that stress can contribute towards a schizoaffective episode. Stress can be caused by many different things, including bereavement or employment problems.

In particular, it is thought that childhood trauma causes the condition to develop in later life. Research shows that bad treatment in your childhood can make psychosis more likely.

There is information on self-help techniques later on in this factsheet. Self-help can help you to manage your symptoms and stress.

You can find out more information on "Does Mental Illness Run in Families?" at www.rethink.org. Or contact our General Enquiries Team on 0121 522 7007 and ask for a copy to be sent to you.

6. HOW IS SCHIZOAFFECTIVE DISORDER TREATED?

National Institute for Health and Care Excellence (NICE) recommends that you should be offered a combination of medication and talking therapies.

NICE create guides for health professionals to follow when treating and caring for a particular condition. The care and treatment for schizoaffective disorder can be found in different guidelines. The most common guidelines used are the following:

- Psychosis and schizophrenia in adults: prevention and management.
- Bipolar disorder: assessment and management.
- Depression in adults: recognition and management.

WHICH MEDICATION WILL I GET?

The medication you are given will depend on the type of schizoaffective disorder you have. Your medication may be a mix of antipsychotics, antidepressants, and mood stabilisers.

- Manic-type schizoaffective disorder is likely to be treated with a mood stabiliser and an antipsychotic drug.
- Depressive type is likely to be treated with a mood stabiliser and antidepressant.
- For an acute episode of schizoaffective disorder, you may be given antipsychotic medication.

An acute episode means that you become very unwell quickly.

Your doctor may also prescribe you sleeping tablets or benzodiazepines. This type of medication is addictive, so you will normally only have them for a short time.

You may forget or not want to take your medication every day. You can ask your doctor about a depot injection instead. You will be given the injection every two or four weeks. You won't have to take tablets if you have a depot injection.

Your doctor may offer you antidepressants. Antidepressants can trigger manic episodes for some people. Your doctor should monitor your medication.

Your GP should consult a psychiatrist if they want to give you an antidepressant alongside another medication such as lithium or antipsychotic medication. Your doctor should do certain checks at certain times to monitor lithium and antipsychotic medication.

WHAT TALKING TREATMENTS SHOULD I GET?

The guidance says the NHS should offer you talking treatments and family intervention as part of your recovery. Cognitive behavioural therapy (CBT) is the main treatment NICE recommends. NICE guidance says that supportive psychotherapy or counselling will not help with psychotic symptoms. But your team should think about your preference and may offer you a different treatment if CBT is not available in your area.

What is CBT?

CBT is a talking treatment. It is there to try and help you to:

- Understand links between your thoughts, feeling, and actions
- Understand your symptoms and how they affect your day-to-day life
- Look at your perceptions, beliefs, and reasoning.

CBT aims to:

- Help you to be aware of signs that your thoughts, feelings, or behaviours are changing
- Give you a way of coping with your symptoms
- Reduce stress and improve your functioning

WHAT IS FAMILY INTERVENTION?

Family intervention is where you and your family work with mental health professionals to help to manage relationships. This should be offered to people who you live with or who you are in close contact with. The support that you and your family are given will depend on what problems there are and what preferences you all have. This could be group family sessions or individual sessions. Your family should get support for

three months to one year and should have at least ten planned sessions.
Family intervention could be to:

- Learn more about your symptoms.
- Improve communication among family members.

Family intervention could help you and your family to:

- Learn more about your symptoms.
- Understand what is happening to you.
- Improve communication with each other.
- Know how to support each other.
- Think positively.
- Become more independent.
- Be able to solve problems with each other.
- Know how to manage a crisis.
- Improve mental wellbeing.

ARTS THERAPY

Arts therapy should be considered for you if your psychosis keeps
coming back. This is known as reoccurring psychosis. Arts therapy may
be more useful if you have depressive symptoms, such as withdrawing
from family and friends.

You will have arts therapy with a therapist. It will usually be in a group.
It is there to mix different communication techniques with creativity.

Art therapy aims to help you to

- Learn new ways of relating to other people.
- Show how you are feeling.
- Accept your feelings.
- Understand your feelings.

You can find more information about

- Antipsychotics
- Antidepressants
- Mood stabilisers
- Benzodiazepines
- Medication—Choice and managing problems
- Talking treatments
- Early intervention
- Crisis teams
- Community mental health teams
- Care programme approach

at www.rethink.org. Or call our General Enquiries team on 0121 522 7007 and ask them to send you a copy of our factsheet.

7. WHO WILL MANAGE MY TREATMENT?

Your GP should refer you to an "early intervention team" after your first psychotic episode. Your GP should not give you antipsychotic medication without first talking to a psychiatrist. You should be assessed quickly.

You will be able to access an early intervention team regardless of your age. Usually you will only be able to access early intervention teams for up to three years. But the team can consider a longer course of therapy if you are still unwell.

If there is not an early intervention team in your area, you should be referred to a crisis team or community mental health team.

These teams are known as "secondary care teams" in the NHS. They are usually made up of psychiatrists, psychologists, mental health nurses, social workers, and support workers. The teams should support you to improve your quality of life. They can support you with things like:

- Treatment options
- Risk of harm to self or others
- Alcohol and drug use

- Your weight
- Smoking
- Nutrition
- Physical activity
- Sexual health
- Relationships
- Accommodation
- Employment
- Education

You may be put under a package of care called the "care programme approach" (CPA). This means that you will have a care plan and care coordinator to make sure that you get the support that you need.

If your symptoms respond well to treatment, you can be referred back to your GP. You should be asked if you are happy for this to happen. Your GP will monitor your symptoms, and will do physical health checks with you.

Your GP may refer you back to secondary care teams if:

- Treatment hasn't helped you to get better.
- You have bad side effects from medication.
- You are misusing alcohol or drugs.
- You are a risk to yourself or other people.

8. WHAT IF I AM NOT HAPPY WITH MY TREATMENT?

If you are not happy with your treatment you can:

- Talk to your doctor about your treatment options.
- Ask for a second opinion.
- Ask a relative, friend, or advocate to help you speak your doctor.
- Contact patient advice and liaison service (pals).
- Make a complaint.

There is more information about these options below.

TREATMENT OPTIONS

You should first speak to your doctor about your treatment.

Explain why you are not happy with it. You could ask what other treatments you could try. Tell your doctor if there is a type of treatment that you would like to try. Doctors should listen to your preference. If you are not given this treatment, ask your doctor to explain why it is not suitable for you.

SECOND OPINION

A second opinion means that you would like a different doctor to give their opinion about what treatment you should have. You can also ask for a second opinion if you disagree with your diagnosis.

You don't have a right to a second opinion. But your doctor should listen to your reason for wanting a second opinion.

ADVOCACY

An advocate is independent from the mental health service. An advocate is free to use. They can be useful if you find it difficult to get your views heard. There are different types of advocates available. Community advocates can support you to get a health professional to listen to your concerns and help you to get the treatment that you would like.

You can search online to search for a local advocacy service. If you can't find a service, you can contact the Rethink Mental Illness Advice Service on 0300 500 927, and we will look for you. But be aware that this type of service doesn't exist in all areas.

THE PATIENT ADVICE AND LIAISON SERVICE (PALS)

PALS is part of the NHS. They give information and support to patients. You can find your local PALS through this website link:

www.nhs.uk/Service-Search/Patient-advice-and-liaison-services-(PALS)/LocationSearch/363.

You can find out more about:

- Medication — Choice and managing problems
- Second opinions
- Advocacy
- Complaining about the NHS or social services

at www.rethink.org. Or call our General Enquiries team on 0121 522 7007 and ask them to send you a copy of our factsheet.

9. WHAT ARE SELF-CARE AND MANAGEMENT SKILLS?

You can learn to manage your symptoms by looking after yourself. Self-care is how you take care of your diet, exercise, daily routine, relationships, and how you are feeling.

PEER SUPPORT AND SELF-MANAGEMENT PROGRAMMES

Peer support means that you get support from other people who also have mental health problems.

- You can get peer support by joining a support group.
- You may be able to get peer support and self-management programmes through your mental health team.

Peer support through the community mental health team should be given by a person who has recovered from psychosis and is well.

Peer support and self-management programmes should give you information and advice about:

- How medication can be helpful.
- Helping you to notice and manage your symptoms.
- How to access mental health support.
- How to access other support services.

- How to cope with stress and other problems.
- What to do in a crisis.
- Help you to build a social support network.
- Help you to notice when you are becoming unwell.
- Help you to set personal recovery goals.

RECOVERY COLLEGE

Recovery colleges are part of the NHS. They offer free courses about mental health to help you manage your symptoms. They can help you to take control of your life and become an expert in your own wellbeing and recovery. You can usually self-refer to a recovery college. But the college may inform your care team.

Unfortunately, recovery colleges are not available in all areas. To see if there is a recovery college in your area you can use a search engine such as Google. Or contact Rethink Mental Illness Advice Service on 0300 5000 927.

MAKE A WELLNESS RECOVERY ACTION PLAN

A Wellness Recovery Action Plan (WRAP) is a plan that you make. The idea of the WRAP is to help you stay well and achieve what you would like to achieve. The WRAP looks at how you are affected by your illness and what you could do to manage it.

There is more information about the WRAP in the further reading section at the end of this factsheet.

10. WHAT RISKS CAN SCHIZOAFFECTIVE DISORDER CAUSE?

The risk of suicide is higher for the first few years after your symptoms start. Seek treatment early and make a crisis plan. The right treatment can help control your symptoms and therefore lower the risk of suicide.

You can make a crisis plan yourself, or you can ask someone to help you. A crisis plan is a plan of action that you will follow to help with suicidal feelings. Usually a plan will include activities that help you to relax, and a list of helpful people who may be your friends, a health professional, or a charity.

You can find out more about **"Suicidal thoughts, how to cope"** at www.rethink.org. Or call our General Enquiries team 0121 522 7007 and ask them to send you a copy of our factsheet.

11. WHAT IF I AM A CARER, FRIEND, OR RELATIVE?

SUPPORT FOR YOU

You can get support if you support someone with schizoaffective disorder. These are some options for you:

- Family Intervention through the NHS
- Join a carers' service
- Join a carers' support group
- Ask your local authority for a carers' assessment
- Read about the condition
- Apply for welfare benefits for carers

SUPPORTING THE PERSON YOU CARE FOR

You might find it easier to support someone with schizoaffective disorder if you understand their symptoms, treatment, and self-management skills.

You should be aware of what you can do if you are worried about their mental state or risk of self-harm. It can be helpful to have at hand contact information for their mental health team or GP. You could find out if your loved one has a crisis plan. You could help your relative to make a crisis plan if they don't have one.

You can find out more information about:

- Supporting someone with a mental illness
- Carer's assessment and support planning
- Benefits for carers
- Getting help in a crisis
- Helping someone with suicidal thoughts
- Responding to unusual thoughts and behaviours
- Confidentiality and information sharing—for carers, friends, and family

at www.rethink.org. Or call our General Enquiries team on 0121 522 7007 and ask them to send you a copy of our factsheet.

WELLNESS RECOVERY ACTION PLAN (WRAP) PLUS. FORMERLY LIVING WITHOUT DEPRESSION AND MANIC DEPRESSION— MARYELLEN COPELAND, PHD.

The Wellness Recovery Action Plan® or WRAP® is a self-designed wellness process. You can use a WRAP to get well, stay well, and make your life your own. It was developed in 1997 by a group of people who were searching for ways to overcome their own mental health issues and move on to fulfilling their life dreams and goals.

Website: http://www.mentalhealthrecovery.com

THE HEARING VOICES NETWORK

This service gives support and understanding for those who hear voices or experience other types of hallucinations.

Telephone: 0114 271 8210

Address: c/o Sheffield Hearing Voices Network, Limbrick Day Service, Limbrick Road, Sheffield, S6 2PE

Email: nhvn@hotmail.co.uk

Website: www.hearing-voices.org

Need more help?
Go to **www.rethink.org** for information on symptoms, treatments, money and benefits and your rights.

Need to talk to an adviser?
If you need practical advice, call us on 0300 5000 927 between 9:30am to 4pm, Monday to Friday. Our specialist advisers can help you with queries like how to apply for benefits, get access to care or make a complaint.

Don't have access to the web?
Call us on 0121 522 7007. We are open Monday to Friday, 9am to 5pm, and we will send you the information you need in the post.

or write to us at Rethink Mental Illness:
RAIS
PO Box 17106
Birmingham B9 9LL

Rethink Mental Illness Advice Service

Phone 0300 5000 927
Monday to Friday, 9:30am to 4pm
(excluding bank holidays)

Email advice@rethink.org

HELPFUL AND FREE— RESOURCES AND GUIDES

HIGHLY RECOMMENDED

Rethink. https://www.rethink.org

Hearing Voices Network. http://www.hearing-voices.org

Bipolar UK. https://www.bipolaruk.org

SUPPORT SERVICES

Below are telephone numbers and website details of support organisations that you may find it beneficial to contact:

TEXT: "SHOUT" TO 85258

- 24/7 UK crisis text service when in need of immediate support

SAMARITANS

- **Phone** 116 123 (24 hours, 7 days a week)
- **www.samaritans.org.uk**

CHILDLINE (FOR CHILDREN AND TEENAGERS)

- Phone 0800 1111
- www.childline.org.uk

ANXIETY UK

Phone 03444 775 774 (Monday to Friday, 9:30 am–5:30 p.m.)
www.anxietyuk.org.uk

SANE LINE

- Phone 0300 304 7000 (every day, 4:30–10:30 pm)
- www.sane.org.uk

CALM (FOR MEN AGED 15 TO 35)

- Phone 0800 58 58 58 (daily, 5 p.m. to midnight)
- www.thecalmzone.net

MIND

- Phone 0300 123 3393 (Monday to Friday, 9a.m.–6p.m.)
- www.mind.org.uk

YOUNG MINDS (INFORMATION ON CHILD AND TEENAGE MENTAL HEALTH, PHONE LINE FOR PARENTS ONLY)

- Phone 0808 802 5544 (Monday to Friday, 9:30 a.m.–4 p.m.)
- www.youngminds.org.uk

CRUSE BEREAVEMENT CARE

- Phone 0808 808 1677 (Monday to Friday, 9 a.m.–5 p.m.)
- www.cruse.org.uk

USEFUL APPS

Mind Shift—Mind Shift is a mental health app designed specifically for teens and young adults with anxiety. Rather than trying to avoid anxious feelings, Mind Shift stresses the importance of changing how you think about anxiety. It can encourage you to take charge of your life, ride out intense emotions, and face challenging situations.

Self Help for Anxiety Management—SAM might be perfect for you if you're interested in self-help and meditation isn't your thing. Users are prompted to build their own 24-hour anxiety toolkit that allows you to track anxious thoughts and behaviour over time, and learn 25 different self-help techniques. You can also use SAM's 'Social Cloud' feature to confidentially connect with other users in an online community for additional support.

Happify—Need a happy fix? With its psychologist-approved mood-training program, the Happify app is your fast-track to a good mood. Try various engaging games, activity suggestions, gratitude prompts and more to train your brain as if it were a muscle, to overcome negative thoughts.

The **Headspace** app makes meditation simple. Learn the skills of mindfulness and meditation by using this app for just a few minutes per day. You gain access to hundreds of meditations on everything from stress and anxiety to sleep and focus. The app also has a handy 'get some headspace' reminder to encourage you to keep practicing each day.

Calm provides people experiencing stress and anxiety with guided meditations, sleep stories, breathing programs, and relaxing music. This app is truly universal; whether you've never tried meditation before or regularly practice, you'll find the perfect program for you.

 **Smiling mind** is a way to practice daily meditation and mindfulness exercises from any device. Smiling Mind is a unique tool developed by psychologists and educators to help bring balance to your life. This is really helpful during times of stress and is a fun and unique way to help you put a smile on your mind ☺

Other NHS approved apps can be discovered here:

https://www.nhs.uk/apps-library/category/mental-health/
There are many other apps you could try which could be helpful but these are some suggestions to try or you may find your own that you like better. There are also many organisations which can provide support which you might find helpful.

LINKS FOR CHILDREN AND TEENAGERS

The below links may be helpful for children or teenagers, or for parents looking for further advice for how to support their child:

https://www.kooth.com
https://www.childline.org.uk
https://youngminds.org.uk
https://www.rcpsych.ac.uk/mental-health/parents-and-young-people
http://www.themix.org.uk

ONLINE SELF-HELP PROGRAMS YOU CAN ACCESS TO HELP SUPPORT YOUR MENTAL HEALTH AND SLEEP

The following links are for online programmes that can help you with a variety of issues including anxiety, low mood, and difficulty sleeping:

https://www.sleepio.com/
https://www.moodjuice.scot.nhs.uk
https://llttf.com
https://www.dbi.scot/aberdeen/
www.beatingtheblues.co.uk

ONLINE SELF-HELP BOOKLETS AND RESOURCES

The online booklets cover a variety of issues, from anxiety to low mood to difficulty sleeping and to loss and bereavement. The booklets provide information about what you may experience if you have any of these difficulties, as well as providing advice for how you may support yourself and manage your situation. The Northumberland Self Help Books (first link) are available in written and audio formats and have large print versions for those who struggle with vision. The final link takes you to some NHS approved audio guides:

https://web.ntw.nhs.uk/selfhelp/
http://wellbeing-glasgow.org.uk/booklets/
https://www.nhs.uk/conditions/stress-anxiety-depression/moodzone-mental-wellbeing-audio-guides/

FURTHER READING

DURING THE COURSE OF THIS book, I have touched on a number of subjects in the fields of mental health and spirituality. For those who would like to look a bit deeper into issues I have highlighted, I have compiled a short reading list to get you started.

Spiritual Assessments in Social Work and Mental Health Practice. David R Hodge (2015) Columbia University Press.
ISBN-13: 978-02311163965

Spirituality and Mental Health. A handbook for service users, carers and staff wishing to bring a spiritual dimension to mental health services. Peter Gilbert. (2011) Pavilion Publishing and Media Ltd.
ISBN: 978-1-908066-00-8

Social Work and Mental Health. Malcolm Golightley. (2010) Learning Matters Ltd.
ISBN-13: 978-1-884445-154-8

Living with Voices. 50 Stories of Recovery. Romme, Escher, Dillon, Corstens, Morris (2015) PCCS Books Ltd.
ISBN: 978 1-906254-22-3

A Straight Talking Introduction to Psychiatric Diagnosis. Lucy Johnson. (2014) PCCS Books Ltd.
ISBN: 978-1-906254-66 7

The Bipolar Disorder Survival Guide. What you and your family need to know. David J Miklowitz, PhD. (2011) The Guilford Press.
ISBN: 978-1-60623-542-3

The Complete Family Guide to Schizophrenia. Muesser, Gingerich (2006) The Guildford Press.
ISBN: 978-1-59385-180-4

Evil Eye, Jinn Possession, and Mental Health: An Islamic Perspective. G Hussein Rassool. (2020) Routledge.
ISBN: 978-0-367-48927-4

Explaining Deliverance. Graham Dow.(1990) Sovereign World Ltd.
ISBN-13: 978-1852400668

Hauntings, Possessions and Exorcisms. Adam C Blai. (2017) Emmaus Road Publishing.
ISBN-13: 978-1945125591

The Social Scientific Study of Exorcism in Christianity. Giordan, Possamai. (2020) Springer.
ISBN-13: 978-3030431723

Walking Out of Spiritual Abuse. Marc Dupont. (1997) Sovereign World.
ISBN: 0-185240-219-9

Father Heart of God. Floyd McClung. (2007) (First published 1985) Kingsway Publications.
ISBN-13: 978-1842913277

Peace with God: The Secret of Happiness. Billy Graham. (2017) TN W Publishing.
ISBN-13: 978-0718088125

REFERENCES

Wikipedia – George Plantagenet, 1st Duke of Clarence.

Wikipedia – Margaret Pole, Countess of Salisbury.

Wikipedia & Wikivisually.com – John Watson (bishop).

Royal Mint – Tower of London Collection 2020.

The Sun – The Ultimate Millionaires' Row – Thomas Burrows 11/10/2018.

Wikipedia – Edward IV.

Historyextra.com – The secret intimacies of Edward IV: multiple marriages and same-sex affair?

The Bible – Isaiah 40:31.

Radical Church Planting. Ellis & Mitchell. 1992.

I am n – Voice of the Martyrs. 2016

Jesus freaks – DC Talk & Voice of the Martyrs. 1999.

RedR UK. 2019.

When Their World Falls Apart. Rosenfeld, Caye, Ayalon & Lahad. 2005.

Social Policy for Development. Hall & Midgley. 2004.

UNICEF. 2005.

Disaster Relief: Models of Community Work. Clarke. 2005.

The Bible – 1 Peter 2:24.

www.hrw.org #break the chains

Foundation Series Vol 1. Derek Prince. 1986.

Hearing Voices Network.

Spiritual Assessments in social Work and Mental Health Practice. Hodge. 2015.

Mental Health Foundation – Hearing Voices.

Social Work and Mental Health – Golightley 2010.

Religion, belief and social work – making a difference. Furnees & Gilligan. 2010.

Merriam-webster.com

Dictionary.com

Collinsdictionary.com

Oxford Languages dictionary – google

Oxford Popular English Dictionary & Thesaurus 2000

www.takingcharge.csh.umn.ed/what-spirituality

Smith Wigglesworth – The secret of His power. Hibbert. 1982.

Christiantoday.com – The man who punched out demons. 2017.

Pigs in the Parlour – A Practical Guide to Deliverance. Hammond. 1973.

Evicting Demonic Squatters & Breaking Bandages. Gibson. 1987.

Walking out of Spiritual Abuse. Dupont. 1997.

Spiritual & Religious Competencies in Clinical Practice. Vieten, Scammell. 2015.

Spirituality, Theology & Mental Health. Cook et al. 2013.

Spirituality & Mental Health. Gilbert at al. 2011.

Spirituality & Mental Health Care. Rediscovering a "Forgotten" Dimension. Swinton. 2001.

Psycho-spiritual Care in Health Care Practice. Harrison et al. 2017.

Psychosis & Spirituality. Consolidating the New Paradigm. Clarke. 2010.

The Bible – Ephesians 3:20.

Royal College of Psychiatrists – www.rcpsych@ac.uk

ABOUT THE AUTHOR

LAURA RUTH – MSC ECON/DIP SW.

Laura has served others in the UK and around the globe. She has worked as: a Missionary, Chaplain, Itinerant Minister, Humanitarian Aid Worker, Motivational Speaker and as a Registered Social Worker in Child Protection and Mental Health. Laura is also an artist.

Lightning Source UK Ltd.
Milton Keynes UK
UKHW011831131121
393907UK00001B/8